Cambridge El

G000124347

Elements in Public and Nonpro
edited by
Andrew Whitford
University of Georgia
Robert Christensen
Brigham Young University

NETWORKS IN THE PUBLIC SECTOR

A Multilevel Framework and Systematic Review

Michael D. Siciliano
University of Illinois Chicago

Weijie Wang
University of Missouri

Qian Hu
University of Central Florida

Alejandra Medina
University of Illinois Chicago

David Krackhardt
Carnegie Mellon University

CAMBRIDGE
UNIVERSITY PRESS

Shaftesbury Road, Cambridge CB2 8EA, United Kingdom

One Liberty Plaza, 20th Floor, New York, NY 10006, USA

477 Williamstown Road, Port Melbourne, VIC 3207, Australia

314–321, 3rd Floor, Plot 3, Splendor Forum, Jasola District Centre, New Delhi – 110025, India

103 Penang Road, #05–06/07, Visioncrest Commercial, Singapore 238467

Cambridge University Press is part of Cambridge University Press & Assessment, a department of the University of Cambridge.

We share the University's mission to contribute to society through the pursuit of education, learning and research at the highest international levels of excellence.

www.cambridge.org
Information on this title: www.cambridge.org/9781009108416

DOI: 10.1017/9781009104241

First published 2022

A catalogue record for this publication is available from the British Library.

ISBN 978-1-009-10841-6 Paperback
ISSN 2515-4303 (online)
ISSN 2515-429X (print)

Networks in the Public Sector

A Multilevel Framework and Systematic Review

Elements in Public and Nonprofit Administration

DOI: 10.1017/9781009104241
First published online: August 2022

Michael D. Siciliano
University of Illinois Chicago

Weijie Wang
University of Missouri

Qian Hu
University of Central Florida

Alejandra Medina
University of Illinois Chicago

David Krackhardt
Carnegie Mellon University

Author for correspondence: Michael D. Siciliano, sicilian@uic.edu

Abstract: Networks contain complex patterns of dependency and require multiple levels of analysis to explain their formation, structure, and outcomes. In this Element, the authors develop the Multilevel Network Framework. The framework serves as (i) a conceptual tool to think more deeply about network dynamics; (ii) a research tool to assist in connecting data, theory, and empirical models; and (iii) a diagnostic tool to analyze and categorize bodies of research. The authors then systematically review the network literature in public administration, management, and policy. They apply the Multilevel Network Framework to categorize the literature; identify significant gaps; examine micro-, macro-, and cross-level relations; and examine relevant mechanisms and theories. Overall this Element helps readers to (i) understand and classify network research, (ii) use appropriate theoretical frameworks to examine network-related problems, (iii) understand how networks emerge and produce effects at different levels of analysis, and (iv) select appropriate empirical models.

Keywords: networks, systematic review, public administration, public policy, governance

ISBNs: 9781009108416 (PB), 9781009104241 (OC)
ISSNs: 2515-4303 (online), 2515-429X (print)

Contents

1 Levels of Analysis and the Multilevel Network Framework

Much of our social, political, and professional lives are motivated and influenced by the relationships we form with others. Networks play a critical role in shaping beliefs and behaviors as they provide the context through which information is acquired, shared meanings develop, activity is coordinated, and norms are established (Coleman, 1990; Friedkin & Johnsen, 2011; McLean, 2017). Given the fundamental role networks play in our lives, researchers have advocated that fields of inquiry adopt a network perspective (Considine et al., 2009; Krackhardt & Brass, 1994; Robins, 2015). A network perspective highlights the importance of social and organizational relationships in shaping individual and collective outcomes. Inherent in the network perspective are micro–macro linkages between social actors and social structures that determine how actors create and are constrained by their social relations (Kilduff & Tsai, 2003, p. 66).

Based on our experiences teaching and conducting network research, we have observed several roadblocks to applying the network perspective. These roadblocks include conceptualizing the specific hypothesis one wants to test, identifying the relevant theory, and selecting the appropriate analytic strategy. These challenges often result in (or are derived from) several sources of confusion prevalent in network studies: (i) a misunderstanding between the unit and level of analysis, (ii) a lack of clarity on the number of observations available for analysis, and (iii) a limited consideration of the mechanisms that influence the relationship of interest.

Consider the following research questions. Why are some nodes more central than others in the network? Which self-organizing behaviors helped produce the observed network's shape? How does an actor's position in the network influence their outcomes? How does the shape of a network affect its overall success? Across these questions, the network serves as both the independent and dependent variable, and the phenomena of interest reside at the nodal, dyadic, and network levels. Just as important, each question draws on a potentially different set of theories linking network phenomena to other individual and group behaviors and outcomes. As Robins (2015, p. 13) notes, one of the strengths and challenges of network research is balancing discussions of individual actors and the social systems they comprise.

We wrote this Element to help scholars and practitioners think more deeply and clearly about networks. This element makes two major contributions. First, this Element contributes to social network research through the development of the Multilevel Network Framework. The framework provides network scholars and practitioners in various fields with an integrated conceptual model to explore how networks form and produce changes in behaviors and outcomes. The framework addresses multiple levels of analysis (nodal, dyadic, and network) and emphasizes the theoretical mechanisms connecting network phenomena within and across those levels. It encourages researchers to articulate more explicitly how different network phenomena of interest are related and reveals gaps in the underlying processes assumed to be at work. This ultimately provides insight into the appropriate data and modeling strategies needed to test theory.

Second, this Element contributes to the fields of public administration, management, and policy more specifically by applying the Multilevel Network Framework as a diagnostic lens. We conduct a systematic review and use the Multilevel Network Framework to categorize and take stock of the existing empirical literature on networks. The framework serves to categorize the extant scholarly research into micro and macro relations, types of variables, and classes of theories and mechanisms applied. Thus, we reveal the range of network relationships our field has emphasized and the significant gaps that remain. This application of the framework leads to the identification of several important areas for future research. Other fields of science can also use the Multilevel Network Framework to explore their progress and identify gaps in their literature. Overall, the framework provides several important roles. It serves as (i) a conceptual tool to help us think more deeply about the nature of network relationships; (ii) a research tool to assist in connecting data, theory, and empirical models; and (iii) a diagnostic tool to analyze and categorize bodies of literature.

This section will describe the development of the Multilevel Network Framework. The framework is based on Coleman's bathtub model (Coleman, 1990) and connects different levels and directions of analysis in network research with relevant mechanisms and theories. Given the framework established in this section, Section 2 provides an overview of the systematic review we conducted of the empirical network literature. Using the Preferred Reporting Items for Systematic reviews and Meta-Analyses (PRISMA) we identified 196 articles in 40 public administration and policy journals between 1998 and 2019. Of the 196 articles that met our search criteria, 107 focused on understanding and modeling the determinants of network formation. The other 89 examined how the composition and structure of the network influenced network effects. Sections 3 and 4 review these articles and integrate the existing network scholarship across various forms and levels.

1.1 What Are Networks?

Before proceeding further, let us begin by defining a network. A network consists of a set of actors or nodes and the links or ties among those actors. The actors in the network can be various entities, including individuals, workgroups, organizations, local governments, and nations. The links connecting the actors can represent a wide range of possible relations. For example, the relations can be (i) social, such as a friend, (ii) interactions, such as advice seeking or communication, as well as (iii) flows, such as the movement of trade, information, or disease (adams, 2020; Borgatti et al., 2013). Networks are most often represented by an adjacency matrix or a graph. For example, Figures 1a and 1b provide both forms of representation for a simple network of ten actors. The actors are labeled A through J.

In Figure 1a, the matrix representation, the rows and columns identify the actors. The intersecting cell for any given row and column indicates the status of the relationship between the corresponding actors. The value of "1" in the matrix means the relationship is present and "0" indicates it is absent. The information contained in the matrix can also be displayed graphically, as seen in Figure 1b. The actors are now represented as nodes, and actors who have a relationship present are connected by an edge or tie in the graph. In Figure 1a, we see that actor E has a tie with actor G, as there is a "1" at the intersection of their row and column. In the graph representation, a corresponding edge connects node E to node G. Networks can be undirected (as in Figures 1a and 1b) or directed, and they can be weighted or binary. In an undirected network, ties are symmetric, such as with collaboration or coauthorship. In a directed network, ties do not need to be symmetric or reciprocal, such as with advice seeking or trade. Weighted networks assign a value to the relationship under study. For example, rather than an advice tie being present or absent, information on the frequency of advice seeking may also be available.

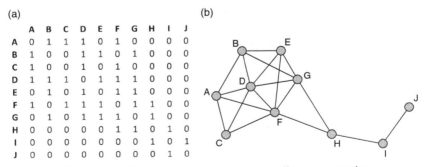

(a)

	A	B	C	D	E	F	G	H	I	J
A	0	1	1	1	0	1	0	0	0	0
B	1	0	0	1	1	0	1	0	0	0
C	1	0	0	1	0	1	0	0	0	0
D	1	1	1	0	1	1	1	0	0	0
E	0	1	0	1	0	1	1	0	0	0
F	1	0	1	1	1	0	1	1	0	0
G	0	1	0	1	1	1	0	1	0	0
H	0	0	0	0	0	1	1	0	1	0
I	0	0	0	0	0	0	0	1	0	1
J	0	0	0	0	0	0	0	0	1	0

(b)

Figure 1 (a) Network represented as an adjacency matrix;
(b) Network represented as a graph

Networks in public administration and policy take on various forms, from interpersonal relationships among street-level workers (Nisar & Maroulis, 2017; Siciliano, 2017) to collaborative agreements among governments (Hugg, 2020; Thurmaier & Wood, 2002). Networks in our field are often described through a variety of names. These names may focus on their function or policy domain, such as a service delivery network (Bunger, 2013; Provan & Milward, 1995) or an economic development network (Lee, 2011). The names may emphasize the nature of the relationships among the actors, such as a communication or advice network (Siciliano, 2015a). Finally, the names may stipulate the presence or absence of an over-arching authority or goal, such as purpose-oriented networks compared to serendipitous ones (Carboni et al., 2019; Nowell & Kenis, 2019; Nowell & Milward, 2022).

Regardless of the name, individual actors (whether humans or organizations) maintain agency over the relationships they form with others. For example, consider the Continuums of Care mandated by the US Department of Housing and Urban Development. The Continuums of Care establish community-wide planning and coordination among nonprofits, government agencies, housing authorities, and school districts. Despite their common origins and mandates, Continuums of Care across the country have been found to vary in their overall structure, the form of governance, size of membership, frequency of advocacy, and strength of relationship with policymakers (Hambrick Jr. & Rog, 2000; Mosley & Jarpe, 2019). Mandates to form networks by an external party (usually a government) may identify sets of actors needed to participate. However, such mandates cannot force those actors to share advice or trust one another (Siciliano, Wang et al., 2021).

Consequently, networks are emergent phenomena, and scholars applying a network perspective often consider the factors that influence tie formation and the implications of those ties. As Krackhardt (2003, p. 330, italics in original) remarks on organizational networks, "An inherent principle of the interactive form is that networks of relations span across the entire organization, unimpeded by preordained formal structures ... These relationships can be multiple and complex. But one characteristic they share is that they *emerge* in the organization, they are not preplanned." Aligned with a network perspective, scholars argue that emergent structures provide greater insight into the functioning of systems and organizations when compared with formal structural variables (Monge & Contractor, 2003, p. 9).

1.2 Units Versus Levels of Analysis

This Element develops a framework for thinking about the micro- and macro-level factors that impact the emergence of ties among actors and how those ties and the resulting network structure produce effects. Underlying the myriad of actors and relations that can comprise networks are multilevel theoretical constructs and mechanisms that help to explain network formation and network effects (Monge & Contractors, 2003). Because networks are multilevel phenomena, research on the same set of actors can operate at different levels of analysis. For example, when studying network performance, at what level does the performance outcome reside? Is it the individual actor's success? Or the community or residents the network is designed to serve (Provan & Milward, 2001)? At the same time, at what level do the factors influencing these outcomes reside? Is it the position of individual nodes that matters? The overall structure of the network? These questions force researchers to understand the distinction between the level of analysis and the unit of analysis in network scholarship.

Traditionally, research does not distinguish between units of analysis and levels of analysis. For example, when we conduct research at the organizational level, this is equivalent to saying our units of analysis are organizations (not individuals in the organization). However, network analysis is different in this regard. Because networks focus on the relationships among entities, not simply their attributes, there is a profound difference between units of analysis and levels of analysis (Krackhardt, 2010). To illustrate this difference, consider Figure 1b, which is a classic "Kite" network (Krackhardt, 1990). Each of the ten nodes in the graph is arbitrarily labeled with a letter. But each node could easily represent a different type of entity. For example, each node could be a person (and the eighteen ties could represent communication ties). Alternatively, each node could be a firm (and each of the eighteen ties could represent interlocking directorship ties). Or, each node could be a country (and each of the eighteen ties could represent bilateral trade agreements). We refer to those different entity types as the units of analysis for the network. The unit of analysis defines the specific scope and content of the nodes in the network.

In contrast, the level of analysis speaks to the structural feature of the graph that corresponds to the research question one is interested in exploring. There are several levels represented in the graph in Figure 1b. For the sake of discussion, let us assume that the unit of analysis is the individual and the ties among those individuals represent "daily communication" links within the team that these ten people belong to. We could be interested in knowing why person H has a tie to person F but not to person D. Or, we could be interested in knowing how H's position in the network gives rise to particular advantages, over and above the advantages enjoyed by D in their position. Or we could be interested in knowing whether the shape of the network, as a whole, contributes to the team's performance. Each of these interests represents a different level of analysis of this one network.

To be specific, the *Level of analysis* in a network study is given by an integer L in the term N^L, where N is the number of nodes in the network and N^L is the potential number of observations that the network provides to address the question. A Level 1 study of this network in Figure 1b would indicate that the primary focus is on the individual node, perhaps the advantages or constraints they experience by occupying their particular position in the network. The number of pertinent observations for such a research question at Level 1 is $N^1 = 10$ in this case; one observation per node in the network. A Level 2 study of this same network might ask the dyadic question, what seems to predict who will communicate with whom in this network? In all, at Level 2, there are N^2 dyadic relations that could be studied. However, as in the case of Figures 1a and 1b, we have imposed symmetry on the ties and do not consider self-relations (people talking to themselves), which reduces our number of observations to $(N^2 - N)/2$. This restriction on the number of possible observations at Level 2 is not unusual, but it still may be thought of as approximating N^2, at least as an order of magnitude estimate.

This same network also permits us to ask another Level question, as mentioned earlier: What is the consequence of the shape of the network as a whole? This is a Level 0 question, where the number of observations provided to address this question is $N^0 = 1$. Thus, despite gathering information on each of the ten actors and their relations, we still have only observed the properties of a single network. Of particular note here is that this Level 0 question is not simply an average of the attributes at the more micro level, Level 1. Rather, the network's shape is defined by a characteristic of the pattern or structure of the network as a whole and cannot be reduced to some sum of its constituent parts.

Finally, to complete our typology of Levels of analysis,[1] we consider that network ties themselves are often perceived differently by different occupants of the system. For example, the fact that H has a tie to I in the Kite network may not be observed by all the other members of the network. If one were to misperceive this critical link, this could affect how they operate within the system. In this context, as Krackhardt (1987) argued, sometimes how people perceive the network can be more critical in terms of their behavior than the actual network in which they are embedded. Level 3 studies allow us to pursue such claims. For example, individuals who are perceived to be central or tied to

---

[1] In addition to the levels mentioned here, network scholars may engage in the analysis of subgroups. Subgroups in networks are defined and calculated in a variety of ways. In general, they can be thought of as sets of actors who are more tightly connected with one another than they are to others in the network. Such groups are identified through the application of detection algorithms, like Girvan–Newman. Subgroup analysis is often conducted as part of an analysis at a particular level. For example, scholars in public administration have used subgroups as a contextual variable in models of nodal behavior (Maroulis, 2017).

prominent actors in the network are also perceived to be higher performers, regardless of their true position (Kilduff & Krackhardt, 1994). Further, individuals with more accurate perceptions of the network have been shown to have greater power and reputations (Kilduff & Krackhardt, 2008; Krackhardt, 1990; Krackhardt & Kilduff, 1999). Thus, analyses of people's perceptions matter because one's view of the broader network shapes their decisions and behaviors. Level 3 analyses focus not on the actual ties between actors but consider all the possible perceptions of ties that could occur between those N actors. The number of observations at Level 3 is N^3 (1,000 in this case, although again, we might only consider the perceptions on symmetric and non-self-communications, which would reduce the number of observations to $N(N-1)N/2 = 450$).

The numeric categorization of the level of analysis is not simply a numeric labeling to separate the different types of research questions that can be posed about a network. The numbers associated with each of the levels create a connection between the structural feature of interest (i.e., nodes or dyads or whole networks) and the number of those structural features available to the researcher for analysis. Another way to summarize this connection is to consider that the level of analysis is also the number of subscripts necessary to refer to the particular observation being referenced. If one is looking at aspects of a whole network, X, then no subscripts are needed to reference it. However, if an analysis is examining the properties of the nodes within the X network, then one needs to identify each of those nodes via a single subscript i, as in X_i. A dyadic, Level 2 analysis likewise requires two subscripts to identify each of the nodes (i and j) involved in a dyad, and thus X_{ij}. Finally, a Level 3 study requires the use of three subscripts as such analyses consider the perception each actor has of the $i–j$ tie, and thus an observation would be referenced as X_{ijk}, where k is the perceiver of the $i–j$ tie.

1.2.1 Methods of Analysis

Each Level of analysis associated with network data requires paying attention to how the individual observations at that level should be treated. While many statistical assumptions can be made at each Level, violations of these assumptions abound and affect the feasibility of particular analytical methods and model choices. In some ways, Level 0 analysis is the easiest, and in some ways, it is the hardest level at which to conduct scientific research. It is easiest because the primary assumption of independence of observations is the most tenable. Most whole networks are treated as if they are independent systems without a structure between the units (i.e., between different networks) that would create an autocorrelation in errors in the models. For example, Crespi

(2020) analyzed a set of over 1,000 hospitals in the United States to show that the average path distance between doctors in their patient-sharing networks within the hospital was significantly related to the hospital's efficiency in delivering health care, controlling for a host of possible confounds. Sarkar et al. (2010) demonstrated across fifty-two bank branches that the shape of the communication networks between informal leaders and other employees explained almost 90 percent of the variance in profitability across those branches. Both studies used traditional statistical tools in their analyses, assuming these organizational units (hospitals and bank branches, respectively) constituted independent observations. The difficulty at this level of analysis is that the data requirements are severe. In the smaller case of the Sarkar et al. study, each of the fifty-two branches required collecting complete network data among each branch's twenty to fifty employees. In the Crespi (2020) study, complete network data were collected for each of the over 1,000 hospitals. This is a cumbersome task, often prohibitively so as the average size of the organizational units increases.

While pursuing network questions at Level 0 is both scientifically interesting and valuable to practitioners, the scope of such studies makes them daunting. Thus, another common approach to dealing with analysis at Level 0 is to conduct case studies, comparing a smaller number of units but fleshing out in detail what is going on in each unit. An excellent example of this is the classic Provan and Milward (1995) study of four community health care systems, wherein they showed that the shape of the networks within each system was related to their overall functioning. Of course, with only four observations, no statistical tests would be sensible. However, their rich description of each system and how these networks related to their daily operations provided compelling evidence and logic for their claims.

For Level 1 analysis, each actor (unit) is ascribed a score based on their position in the network. An immediate advantage that Level 1 studies have is that there are N observations for each network, making such studies much more amenable to statistical inferential tests than Level 0. Within the study of organizations, Burt's (1992) development of "structural holes" is a prominent concept, both theoretically and empirically. In Level 1 studies, each actor's structural position is measured, along with other variables that can also be attributed to the actor. Again, traditional econometric methods are frequently used in such analyses, treating each actor in the network as an independent observation.

While traditional econometrics is the most common analysis approach at Level 1, one could argue that these units are not independent of one another, an assumption that is essential to statistical testing. Indeed, the fact that critical network ties are part of the theoretical story by itself might encourage the researcher to question whether this assumption is valid. Fortunately, network autocorrelation models have been developed (Doreian et al., 1984; Leenders, 2002) to test these assumptions, assess the strength of this lack of independence, and control for it to the extent it affects the observations of interest. If the data are longitudinal, then even more sophisticated methods can be used to tease apart the various sources of influence over time (Snijders, 2017).

Level 2 questions, however, are unambiguously non-independent. No one would try to defend the N^2 observations available among N actors as statistically independent of one another. Indeed, Krackhardt (1988) showed that treating Level 2 observations as independent when in fact there may only exist a moderate degree of interdependence leads to large Type I errors in statistical testing. In a set of simulations, he demonstrated that more than half of the simulated samples "appear" statistically significant when in fact the samples were drawn from a population where the null hypothesis is true.

Two streams of work have been shown to deal with this problem with Level 2 data. The first, the Quadratic Assignment Procedure (QAP), applies a permutation test, which has been shown to be robust against the extent of interdependence among observations (Dekker et al., 2007; Krackhardt, 1988). The second is a larger body of work, called Exponential Random Graph Models (ERGM), that approaches this problem from a stochastic viewpoint (Lusher et al., 2013; Robins et al., 1999). Both methods allow the researcher to pursue Level 2 questions while explicitly acknowledging the lack of independence in the raw dyadic data. Methods for longitudinal data have been developed for ERGMs (Cranmer et al., 2021), as well as stochastic actor-oriented models (SAOM) as implemented through RSiena (Ripley et al., 2022). Depending on the granularity of the data, relation event models (REM) have been developed to deal with time-stamped dyadic data (Butts, 2008).

Level 3 questions, where there are three actors associated with each observation (a perceiver, a sender, and a receiver of a tie), compound this lack of independence problem exponentially. If we want to know the answer to the question, why does John think that Sue is a friend of Robert, there are so many sources of confound here that it is difficult to even think about how to model them. As a result, what scholars have done instead is aggregate Level 3 data to a higher level. For example, Krackhardt (1990) asked, do people with more accurate perceptions accrue more power in the organization? By comparing Level 3 data on an actor's perception of the whole network with a Level 2 assessment of the "actual" network, he computed an accuracy score for each network actor. He then used traditional econometric methods to answer the accuracy-power question. Almost all the empirical work with Level 3 data has aggregated up to either

Level 2 or Level 1 observations, as Krackhardt did, to get an answer to the question of interest. However, these aggregations leave the fundamental Level 3 questions on the table: Why do some people perceive some actors to send some ties to other specific actors? And while scholars are working on possible modeling approaches to address these questions, there is, to date, no peer-reviewed or generally accepted statistical techniques to deal with these thorny Level 3 issues.

1.2.2 Direction of Analysis

Another layer of complexity when studying networks is the direction of analysis. Like other phenomena, networks can serve as both (i) dependent variable, where the ties and overall shape of the network are to be explained, and (ii) independent variable, where the network explains some other outcome. Combining the level of analysis with the direction of analysis, we create a 4×2 table that depicts the type of research questions that can be asked at that level and direction of analysis. Table 1 provides sample research questions for each cell, along with examples of typical methods of analysis.

1.3 Framework Overview

The Multilevel Network Framework shown in Figure 2 serves to combine the level and direction of analysis along with linkages that serve as placeholders for the relevant mechanisms and theories that connect the variables under study. The model is based on Coleman's bathtub, also known as Coleman's boat (Coleman, 1990). Coleman's bathtub model has been used in a variety of fields interested in relating micro-level events to macro-level structures and outcomes. The bathtub model "provides a systematic scheme for articulating social explanations and their presuppositions" (Ylikoski, 2016, p. 3). Consequently, the model forces a researcher to be explicit about the processes and mechanisms that give rise to the phenomenon of interest.

In our adaptation, the Multilevel Network Framework combines two bathtub diagrams and situates the network (its shape and composition) at the center. The network, Point D in Figure 2, serves to connect the two bathtubs together. On the left side is a model of network formation, consisting of Points A, B, and C. This side of the framework treats the network as the dependent variable and focuses on processes of network formation. On the right side of the framework, the network functions as the independent variable and connects with Points E, F, and G. This side of the framework examines the implications and consequences of network structure. Each point in the framework is also associated with a particular level of analysis (nodal, dyadic, and network). Note, we do not include the cognitive level (Level 3) in the framework, though one could imagine extending the model

Table 1 Sample research questions at different levels and direction of analysis

Level of analysis	Number of observations (directed network)	Network as dependent variable (network formation)	Network as independent variable (network effects)
Level 0 (Network Level)	N^0	*Research Question*: Why are some networks more centralized than others?	*Research Question*: Are more densely connected networks higher performing?
Whole network structure/ group outcomes		*Typical Methods*: Case Studies or when enough observations of independent networks exist, standard statistical models.	*Typical Methods*: Case Studies or when enough observations of independent networks exist, standard statistical models.
Level 1 (Nodal Level)	N^1	*Research Question*: Which nodal attributes are most predictive of centrality?	*Research Question*: Are nodes with higher betweenness centrality more likely to be innovative?
Actor position/Actor outcomes		*Typical Methods*: Standard statistical models.	*Typical Methods*: Standard statistical models; network autocorrelation models.
Level 2 (Dyad Level)	$\sim N^2$	*Research Question*: Does homophily lead to tie formation?	*Research Question*: Do connected nodes maintain similar beliefs or display similar behaviors?

Table 1 (cont.)

Level of analysis	Number of observations (directed network)	Network as dependent variable (network formation)	Network as independent variable (network effects)
Partner Selection/Contagion		*Typical Methods*: QAP, ERGM, SAOM, REM.	*Typical Methods*: Common to aggregate dyadic effects in this cell to the nodal level and use network autocorrelation models. Co-evolutionary SAOMs are also used with longitudinal data.
Level 3 (Cognitive Level)	$\sim N^3$	*Research Question*: Why do some nodes believe that particular others trust a leader?	*Research Question*: How does the manipulation of beliefs about ties create political advantages?
Network perceptions		*Typical Methods*: Under development. In general, mixed methods incorporating controls for lack of independence in observations.	*Typical Methods*: Under development. In general, mixed methods incorporating controls for lack of independence in observations.

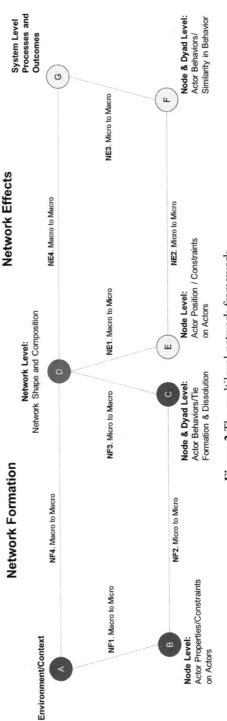

Figure 2 The multilevel network framework

downward to incorporate cognitive perceptions. Notably, as shown in Section 2, no study conducted research at the cognitive level in our systematic review. A point we return to in Section 5.

Each of the seven points in the framework is connected by links. We label each of the links in the framework based on (i) the direction of analysis, network formation (NF) or network effects (NE), and (ii) a number to represent the specific link. The labeling of the links 1, 2, 3, and 4 parallel Coleman's original figure as well as common usage of the bathtub model in organization and sociology literatures. Hence, we maintain this nomenclature to be consistent with prior work. To further maintain consistency, we consider nodal (Level 1) and dyadic (Level 2) variables as micro-level variables and network variables (Level 0) as macro-level variables. Each of the labeled links indicates the relevant bathtub in the framework, network formation (NF), or network effects (NE) along with the relation of interest (1, 2, 3, or 4). Thus, NF1 refers to the relation linking the context or environment of a network to the properties of the actors. In sum, NF1 and NE1 depict macro–micro relations, NF2 and NE2 depict micro–micro relations, NF3 and NE3 depict micro–macro relations, and NF4 and NE4 depict macro–macro relations.

The links represent the relevant theory and mechanisms that operate and allow certain variables in the framework to influence or produce the phenomena at other points. Sections 2 and 3 will cover these links in more detail and discuss existing literature that falls on each of these paths. For now, we will begin with a definition of each point and its level of analysis. Following the definitions, an example of a complete theoretical story spanning both the network formation and network effects bathtubs will be provided to stitch all the different aspects of the framework together.

Point A. Point A consists of the environmental and institutional context in which actors operate. This context could be captured by policy domain (e.g., emergency management vs. education), organizational climate, or other macro-social conditions that may influence individual actors. In situations of collaborative governance, the rules and processes established by the collaborative (Emerson & Nabatchi, 2015) could be Point A features. These features operate at Level 0, as there is one observation or value per network.

Point B. Point B refers to the resources, attributes, preferences, beliefs, and motivations of the actors that may be influenced by the context or environment in which they operate. These are Level 1 variables. For instance, under organizational climates that are less psychologically safe, individuals may be less motivated to discuss errors with others for fear of being reprimanded (Edmondson, 1999). However, contexts and environments certainly do not determine all influences at

Point B. Actors possess various attributes and characteristics that also influence beliefs and motivations that ultimately influence Point C phenomena.

Point C. Point C refers to the behavior of the actors. Here we are interested in examining the dyadic choices and actions taken by the network members. Given our focus on networks as the dependent variable on the framework's left side, we emphasize the actors' tie formation and tie dissolution decisions. In other words, who do actors form relationships with, who do they avoid relationships with, and which existing relations do they choose to dissolve? The behavior of interest at Point C is primarily dyadic (Level 2). However, one could focus solely on individual behavior if the interest is in the general outgoingness of actors rather than a specific set of dyadic relationships.

Point D. At the center of the diagram is Point D. This point captures the shape of the network, a Level 0 variable, resulting from the tie formation and tie dissolution decisions of the actors in the network. Several important network shapes have been discussed in the literature. These include core-periphery structures, E–I index, centralization, small-world networks, and Krackhardt's graph theoretic dimensions (Krackhardt, 1994). Point D plays a unique role in the diagram because it is at once the final point in the process of linkages leading to a network of relations among actors and the macro entity that also creates opportunities and constraints for those actors. Thus, while the shape of the network emerges through the decisions of individual actors, the shape subsequently influences the behavior and performance of the actors in the network.

Point E. Point E refers to an individual actor's position in the network (e.g., their closeness centrality) as well as the constraints and opportunities that may arise due to that position or the overall shape of the network. Point E can also consider other aspects of an actor's network, such as the composition of their peers or the amount of social support received from their relationships. These are Level 1 variables because there is one measure per actor in the network. To observe or calculate structural variables at Point E, one typically needs data on the broader network as depicted at Point D.

Point F. Point F captures the behaviors and attitudes of the individual actors. Unlike Point C, these behaviors are not focused on tie formation and dissolution but rather any behavior of interest to public administration, management, and policy scholars. Such behaviors could include turnover intention, prosocial behaviors, corruption, and performance, among others. The primary scholarly interest is in understanding how an actor's position may affect their behavior. For example, Burt (2004) posited that individuals who bridge otherwise disconnected actors have better information and performance than those who do not. Individual node performance is a Level 1 variable. Scholars also investigate Level 2 phenomena at Point F when considering the similarity in actor preferences, attitudes, or behaviors.

Point G. Point G constitutes the system-level or macro-level outcomes that may emerge through individual behaviors. However, point G is more than the simple aggregation of individual behaviors. In fact, the phenomena observed at point G may not be intended by any individual's behavior (Coleman, 1990). A classic example of how individual actions can lead to emergent phenomena is Schelling's (1971) model of racial segregation. Point G, because it captures the performance and outcomes of the network, resides at Level 0. There is only a single observation of any given network's performance.

1.3.1 Complete Theoretical Story

To help relate all the points in the framework together, we offer a complete story covering both sides of the framework. The context for the story is a traditional Weberian bureaucracy consisting of several work units or departments. A summary of this story mapped to the Multilevel Network Framework is depicted in Figure 3.

The story concerns how the shape of an organization's friendship network may influence the ability of the organization to respond to various crises (Krackhardt & Stern, 1988). We begin on the left side of the model at Point A. Here we have an organization that has implemented several competition-based strategies designed to improve performance. Because the strategies are organization-wide, they are considered a Level 0, macro phenomena. These strategies could include performance evaluations with forced distributions resulting in high and low-performing work units, unit-based recognition awards, contests between units, published rankings of unit performance, or merit pay given to members of top-performing units (Pfeffer & Sutton, 2000). These common management practices may produce work environments that create, at Point B, a strong ingroup vs. outgroup dynamic, leading to perceptions of competition for resources (Deutsch, 1949; Siciliano, 2015a). Given strong associations to one's own work unit and a sense of competition to other units, individuals may tend to form homophilous friendship ties based on work unit. Thus, at Point C, the dyadic friendship choices of individuals will tend to favor those in their own unit. As dyadic ties form predominately within a unit, the overall structure of the network will be one in which there are very few cross-unit relationships. This results in a network shape at Point D with a negative E–I index. The E–I index is measured as:

$$E - I \text{ Index} = \frac{EL - IL}{EL + IL}$$

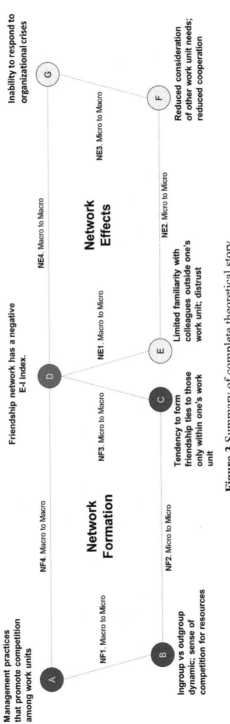

Figure 3 Summary of complete theoretical story

Management practices that promote competition among work units

NF1. Macro to Micro

Network Formation

NF4. Macro to Macro

Friendship network has a negative E-I index.

NF3. Micro to Macro

NF2. Micro to Micro

Ingroup vs outgroup dynamic; sense of competition for resources

Tendency to form friendship ties to those only within one's work unit

NE1. Macro to Micro

NE4. Macro to Macro

Network Effects

NE2. Micro to Micro

NE3. Micro to Macro

Limited familiarity with colleagues outside one's work unit; distrust

Inability to respond to organizational crises

Reduced consideration of other work unit needs; reduced cooperation where EL is the number of external (outside of unit) friendship links and IL is the number of internal (within a unit) friendship links. The E–I index is an important network level (Level 0) summary of the network's shape. It measures the dominance of external ties over internal ties (Krackhardt & Stern, 1988) rather than a simple sum of the number of external ties. The index ranges from −1 (all internal ties) to +1 (all external ties).

The right side of the framework now concerns how the E–I index of the friendship network affects an organization's ability to respond to crises. Based on identity theory, social structures with a low E–I index foster strong loyalty and identity to one's own unit (Point E). However, when crises arise in a low E–I index organization, the lack of cross-unit ties leads individuals to not look for solutions to the larger problem confronting the organization. Instead, the focal group for strategy seeking and crisis management becomes the local work unit, not the organization as a whole. Consequently, behavior at Point F demonstrates a lack of consideration of the needs and concerns of those in other units. In contrast, as the number of ties spanning work units increases, the salient group one identifies with becomes the larger organization. This facilitates problem-solving at the collective rather than local level. Thus, limited friendship across organizational boundaries leads to a reduced system-level (Point G) capacity to respond to crises.

Overall, the Multilevel Network Framework is designed to function as a tool for thinking about network theory and the practical implications such theorizing implies. For example, take the sample research question in Table 1 about why some networks are more centralized than others. This is a question that falls on the left side of the framework concerning network formation. Research on network formation often posits tendencies toward centralization. However, such structural phenomena can arise through various mechanisms ranging from boundedly rational individuals attempting to minimize search costs to endogenous network-level self-organization through preferential attachment. If, for instance, a regional service delivery network aimed to become more centralized, what strategies could they pursue in order to do so? Answering such a question relies on understanding the mechanisms that operate in forming the network.

Similarly, centralized networks are often considered essential drivers of network performance. This relationship is about network effects, where the network serves as the independent variable (right side of the framework). Several studies have identified a positive association between network centralization and performance (Akkerman et al., 2012; Markovic, 2017; Provan & Milward, 1995). But how exactly does the centralization of a network translate into higher performance? Is there a macro-level relationship between centralization and performance (along link NE4 connecting network shape directly to network-level effects), or do centralized networks shape the behavior of the individual nodes in ways that are beneficial for the collective (an effect that would follow links NE1 – NE2 – NE3; thus, linking network shape to individual constraints/benefits to individual behaviors to collective outcomes)?

The remainder of this Element digs further into these issues and summarizes the existing literature in public administration and policy. Section 2 summarizes the systemic review undertaken to identify the relevant network literature. Section 3 examines the studies that treat networks as the dependent variable (network formation) and Section 4 explores research where the network serves as the independent variable (network effects). Finally, Section 5 summarizes the findings and identifies avenues for future network scholarship.

2 Systematic Review Process and Findings

Section 1 developed a framework for thinking through the various levels and determinants of network formation and the structural and compositional drivers of network effects. Table 1 provides intuition behind the number of observations available to test a specific hypothesis and, given the dependencies inherent in network data, the suitable methods for doing so. This section provides an overview of the systematic review process we undertook to gather relevant public administration, management, and policy literature and provides a summary description of that literature. In Sections 3 and 4, we then apply the Multilevel Network Framework to understand the level and direction in which our field has been examining network processes. This application of the Multilevel Network Framework in Sections 3 and 4 will (i) provide further insight into each of the links in the framework, (ii) demonstrate how scholars use theory to connect variables at different levels, and (iii) identify areas with limited scholarship.

We implemented a slightly modified version of the Preferred Reporting Items for Systematic reviews and Meta-Analyses (PRISMA) protocol (Moher et al., 2009) to identify the relevant literature in public administration and policy. Rather than engaging in a broad search of all possible journals and papers, we began by initially bounding our search to forty core journals in public administration and policy. Scholars previously identified these journals based on mission statements, bibliometrics, and perceptions of journal editors (Bernick & Krueger, 2010; Forrester & Watson, 1994; Kapucu et al., 2017). See Table 2 for a list of journals and the number of relevant articles identified from each.[2]

---

[2] This systematic review is part of a larger project that has, at of the time of publication of this Element, produced two published articles and one other working paper. These manuscripts will be cited below as they provide a detailed discussion of the use of different theories of network formation (Siciliano, Wang, et al., 2021), network effects (Medina et al., 2021), the evidence linking different structural features of networks to various outputs and outcomes (Hu et al., 2022).

Table 2 Article count by journal

Journal	Network formation articles	Network effects articles
Administration and Society	3	4
The American Review of Public Administration	6	6
Australian Journal of Public Administration	1	1
Canadian Public Administration	0	0
Evaluation Review	1	0
Financial Accountability and Management	0	0
Human Relations	2	1
International Journal of Public Administration	2	2
International Review of Administrative Sciences	1	0
Journal of Accounting and Public Policy (JAPP)	0	0
Journal of Health Politics, Policy, and Law (JHPPL)	0	2
Journal of Management Studies	1	3
Journal of Policy Analysis &Management	0	3
Journal of Public Administration Research and Theory	13	17
Journal of Public Budgeting, Accounting & Financial Management	0	0
Journal of Public Policy (JPP)	6	2
Journal of Urban Affairs (UA)	5	3
Municipal Finance Journal	0	0
National Tax Journal	0	0
Nonprofit Management and Leadership	2	2
Nonprofit and Voluntary Sector Quarterly	8	4
Organization Studies	2	4
Policy Sciences	0	1
Policy Studies Journal	19	8
Political Psychology Journal	0	0

Table 2 (cont.)

Journal	Network formation articles	Network effects articles
Political Science Quarterly	0	0
Public Administration & Development	0	1
Public Administration	3	5
Public Administration Quarterly	0	1
Public Administration Review	15	5
Public Budgeting and Finance	0	0
Public Finance Review	0	0
Public Performance and Management Review	2	2
Publius	1	0
Review of Policy Research	3	5
Review of Public Personnel Administration	0	0
State and Local Government Review	1	0
Social Science Quarterly	1	0
Urban Affairs Review	8	0
Public Management Review	1	7
Total	107	89

Our systematic review covered the period from January 1998 to the end of May 2019. The starting year of 1998 was chosen for several reasons. First, models for network tie formation capable of effectively dealing with issues of dependency in network data were just being developed (Anderson et al., 1999; Wasserman & Pattison, 1996). These models, known as exponential random graph models (ERGM), are a primary tool for researchers interested in understanding the processes and drivers of network formation (Level 2 questions). Second, around the same time, a Windows version of the UCINET software was released, offering scholars easier access to network analysis tools. Finally, 1998 was previously selected as a starting date by other scholars conducting assessments on the use of network analysis methods in public administration and policy (Kapucu et al., 2017).

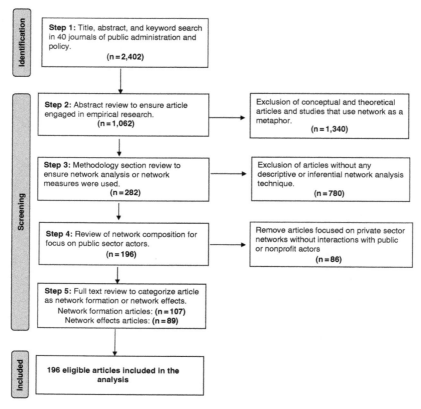

Figure 4 PRISMA flow chart

Figure 4 presents the specific steps of the PRISMA protocol used to identify articles using network analysis in public administration and policy journals. The process began by going to the homepage of each journal and conducting a keyword search. The keywords used were "network," "network analysis," "collaboration," and "collaborative." Next, we searched for each word and combination of words in the title, abstract, and keywords. This search process across all forty journals resulted in 2,402 articles. We then reviewed each abstract to ensure the article engaged in empirical research. Our definition of empirical research included descriptive papers, case studies, statistical analyses, and qualitative methods. The abstract review eliminated 1,340 articles that focused on networks as a metaphor or theoretical concept. We then read the methodology section of each of the remaining 1,062 articles to ensure the authors gathered network data and used network-related measures in their analysis. This step removed an additional 780 articles. The remaining 282 were then examined to ensure a focus on public sector networks and public sector actors (including nonprofits). Based on this criterion, we removed eighty-six articles that focused on private-sector networks. Finally, we reviewed the remaining 196 articles to determine the direction of analysis. Each manuscript was then categorized as being focused on either network formation or network effects. We found 107 articles on network formation (left side of the Multilevel Network Framework) and 89 articles on network effects (right side of the Multilevel Network Framework).

We systematically coded a range of article-specific information for the 196 articles (107 network formation and 89 network effects) that met our search and inclusion criteria. Our coding included information on the policy domain, the type of network data, the primary level of analysis (based on the dependent variable), the type of nodes in the network, the number of networks in the study, the number of time points, and the primary tie type or relationship studied. The coding process began by having three members of the research team code a pilot set of twenty articles. We used the pilot to standardize coding procedures and identify and fix any issues with the protocol. Once the pilot study was complete, two coders independently coded each of the remaining articles. All coding decisions were reviewed, and any inconsistencies were flagged and resolved by group consensus. Table 3 provides a summary of the article-level information we coded. The findings are separated based on the direction of analysis: network formation vs. network effects. While eighty-nine articles on network effects met our search and inclusion criteria, only seventy-four were used for analysis. Fifteen articles were removed due to a lack of network effect data as the text of the article contained insufficient information to code several variables of interest.

The domains covered by research on network effects and network formation are relatively similar in percentages. Both directions of research have emphasized environmental management and economic development, while network effects research has conducted a more significant portion of work on education. Regarding node type, both network effects and network formation research has prioritized the study of networks where organizations, rather than individuals, are the nodes. This finding aligns with previous reviews of network research in public administration (Kapucu et al., 2017). The networks analyzed in public administration and policy are typically captured at only a single time point. Nearly 80 percent of network formation research and 87 percent of network effects research have been cross-sectional. Only nine network formation studies and three network effects studies have analyzed networks at three or more time points.

The number of networks needed for a study can be affected by several factors. One critical factor is the level of the research question or hypothesis.

Table 3 Descriptive information for articles in systematic review

Variable	Categories	Number of network formation articles (percent)	Number of network effects articles (percent)
Domains	Environmental management	25 (23.4%)	15 (20%)
	Health and human services	16 (15%)	13 (18%)
	Education	9 (8.4%)	11 (15%)
	Emergency Management	15 (14%)	9 (12%)
	Community and Economic development	19 (17.7%)	9 (12%)
	Other	23 (21.5%)	17 (23%)
Node type	Individuals	24 (22.4%)	21 (28%)
	Organizations	75 (70.1%)	47 (64%)
	Both	8 (7.5%)	5 (6.7%)
	Other (e.g., countries)	0 (0.0%)	1 (1.3%)
Time points	One	83 (77.6%)	64 (87%)
	Two	15 (14%)	7 (10%)
	Three	5 (4.7%)	1 (1%)
	Four	0 (0.0%)	1 (1%)
	Five or more	4 (3.7%)	1 (1%)
Level of Analysis (based on the primary dependent variable)	Level 0 – Network	38 (35.5%)	40 (54%)
	Level 1 – Nodal	8 (7.5%)	28 (38%)
	Level 2 – Dyadic	61 (57%)	6 (8%)
	Level 3 -Cognitive	0 (0%)	0 (0%)
Type of Relationship	Instrumental	93 (86.9%)	65 (88%)
	Formal	12 (11.2%)	6 (8%)
	Affective	2 (1.9%)	2 (3%)
	Other	0 (0%)	1 (1%)

Table 3 (cont.)

Variable	Categories	Number of network formation articles (percent)	Number of network effects articles (percent)
Number of Networks[a]	1	65 (60.7%)	40 (54%)
	2–10	34 (31.8%)	20 (27%)
	11–98	1 (0.9%)	10 (14%)
	>100	0 (0%)	1 (1%)

([a]For the network effects articles, there are three ego-network studies not accounted for in this group; therefore, the total number is 71. For the network formation articles, there are seven ego-network studies not considered in this group; therefore, the total number of studies is 100).

As discussed in Section 1, questions or hypotheses at Level 2, the dyadic level, have the greatest number of observations (ignoring Level 3 for now, given its lack of attention in the literature) and thus can often be addressed with data from a single network. However, some questions or hypotheses are at Level 0, and therefore, only a single observation is available per network. In these instances, inferential analysis of macro-level phenomena would require data from a large number of networks. One of the longstanding challenges with network research is the difficulty of collecting data on more than one network. That difficulty arises, in part, because of the need for high response rates for valid network measurement. Further, gathering data on multiple networks often also entails developing relationships in multiple settings. For instance, a scholar interested in studying the communication ties among local government employees would need to build relationships with each government of interest. Consequently, it is not surprising that most network studies to date only involve a single network. As Table 3 shows, over 60 percent of the network formation studies and 54 percent of the network effects studies involved a single network. Only around 7 percent of all network research has been conducted on more than ten networks. Methodological developments in text analysis and data mining can facilitate data collection efforts on larger numbers of networks (Berardo et al., 2020).

The ties or relationships among the nodes in a network can vary considerably. Ties can constitute instrumental (e.g., advice seeking, communication), formal (e.g., contracts, trade agreements), affective (e.g., trusts, likes, dislikes), and other relationship types. Despite the variety of ties that connect nodes in networks, nearly 90 percent of all networks studied in our field have been focused on instrumental ties. This is surprising given how common the analysis of friendship networks is in the broader network literature. While studies in public administration and policy do not focus on modeling friendship tie formation, studies have measured the existence of friendship among the actors. For instance, Siciliano (2015a) used friendship ties to predict instrumental ties, suggesting that friendship ties may lead to advice ties. Thus, the coding of the relationship type in Table 3 indicates the primary relationship of interest in the study, for example, the specific tie type being modeled as the dependent variable.

Finally, and most relevant for the Multilevel Network Framework, is the level of analysis. Here we find a significant difference between network formation and network effects studies in terms of Level 1 and Level 2 studies. Network formation studies, given their emphasis on the tie choices of the nodes, have placed a greater focus on Level 2 analyses. While network effects studies, interested in the implications of network structures and positions, have focused more on Level 1 analyses. No network formation or network effects study examined Level 3 data or questions – an issue we discuss in more detail in Section 5.

2.1 Theories and Mechanisms Used to Predict Network Formation and Network Effects

One of the primary goals of this Element is to help researchers and practitioners think more deeply about the mechanisms that may be operating at various levels to form or dissolve ties and to translate network properties into various outputs and outcomes. To that end, we consider the variety of theories and mechanisms scholars have used to understand and predict network formation and network effects. Beyond the coding of the article-level features noted in Table 3, we also extracted and coded each network-based hypothesis in the articles based on the theory or mechanism used by the authors to associate the independent and dependent variables. Not every article obtained from the systematic review contained testable hypotheses. Several of the articles meeting our review criteria were descriptive or did not provide specific hypotheses. Thus, hypotheses were only extracted from the inferential articles seeking to test explicit hypotheses. Out of the 107 network formation articles, 72 were inferential, and of the 74 network effects articles suitable for analysis, 56 were inferential.

The process began by initially open coding the relevant information for each hypothesis. We captured the exact text of the hypothesis, the theoretical mechanism used by the authors to frame and support the hypothesis, the author's description of how the mechanism works, and the link in the Multilevel Network Framework along which the hypothesis operated. Given the different directions of analysis between network formation, where the network is the dependent variable, and network effects, where the network is the independent variable, the open mechanism/theory codes for each type of study were analyzed separately.

Four research team members worked iteratively to develop and categorize the open codes into their appropriate theoretical buckets. For example, in the network effects literature, Jokisaari and Vuori (2009) hypothesized that organizations with lower constraint (i.e., higher brokerage) are more likely to be early adopters of new practices. Marcum et al. (2012, p. 523) argued that the control afforded to a given actor in a network will be positively related to the "number of pairs of organizations to which it is directly tied and which are not directly tied to one another." Both of these hypotheses focus on the role of bridging social capital and the informational or control benefits that often accrue to actors in brokerage or bridging roles. Thus, both hypotheses belong to the larger theoretical category we labeled 'Social Capital – Bridging/Brokerage/ Structural Holes.'

Once the team identified the set of general categories, two teams of coders recoded each hypothesis into its proper category. Each hypothesis was coded into a single category. In making our designation, we relied on the authors' description of the hypothesis and how they built support and provided rationale for the association between the independent and dependent variables. As with the article-level coding, all coding decisions for the hypotheses were compared, and disagreements were brought to the larger team to reach a consensus. In total, we coded 266 hypotheses from the network formation articles and 223 hypotheses from network effects articles. The following sections provide an overview of the relevant theories and their frequency in network formation and network effects research.

2.1.1 Theories on Network Formation

Table 4 provides a list and brief description of each of the theoretical categories and mechanisms identified in the network formation articles and the number of times that mechanism was used to support a hypothesis. For more information and an in-depth discussion of each mechanism associated with network formation, see Siciliano, Wang, et al. (2021). Building off the work of Contractor et al. (2006), the fifteen categories identified were separated into two classes. The first class consists of general social science theories associated with actor incentives and constraints on tie formation behavior. While applied to network formation

Table 4 Theories and mechanisms of network formation (adapted from Siciliano, Wang et al., 2021).

Theoretical category/ mechanism	Description	Number of hypotheses
General social theories		
Collaboration Risk/Risk Hypothesis	Risks associated with division, defection, and coordination.	17
Social Capital – Bridging	Interest in forming bridging ties and connecting to those with novel information or ideas.	13
Social Capital – Bonding	Interest in forming close, dense networks for additional support or the ability to sanction those who defect.	16
Social Capital – Trust	Trust as a precondition for tie formation; or seeking ties to trusted actors.	15
Resource Dependence Theory	How power, resource needs, or dependency on others for resources shapes one's networking behavior.	22
Transaction Costs	The search, bargaining, and policing costs to an agreement or relationship.	6
Rational Choice/Cost-Benefit Calculations	The rational decisions of actors who weigh the benefits against costs when deciding to form a relationship.	15
Homophily – Attribute-Based	Connecting with others who share or are similar to you in terms of attributes.	31
Homophily – Geography Based	Connecting with others who are close to you in terms of physical distance or space.	6
Heterophily/ Heterogeneity	Interest or value in connecting to others who are unlike yourself.	4

Table 4 (cont.)

Theoretical category/ mechanism	Description	Number of hypotheses
Network-Specific/ Endogenous		
Transitivity/Triadic Closure	Tendency for actors with a common third partner to also be connected.	9
Reciprocity	Mutuality; situations where the two members of a dyad each send a tie to the other.	10
Preferential Attachment	Tendency to partner with already popular actors. Also known as the Mathew effect or the "rich get richer".	9
Multiplexity	Social relations tend to overlap. Ties in of one type are likely predictive of or correlated with ties of another.	6
Other/NA		
Other	Any other mechanism not listed above. This group includes hypotheses on bargaining, cognitive consistency theory, and social interdependence.	12
NA	No explicit theory provided; hypothesis typically supported based on context and setting.	75

hypotheses in the literature we reviewed, these mechanisms can also operate in non-network analysis settings or be considered exogenous to the network itself. In terms of network formation research, we use the term exogenous to refer to variables that may reside at Points A (environment/context) and B (actor properties) in the Multilevel Network Framework and thus do not depend on the network for their measurement. The second class of mechanisms is what we refer to as network-specific mechanisms, which are often focused on endogenous or self-organizing properties of networks. Endogenous or self-organization in this context refers to how specific structural properties of the network or its sub-structures may influence the likelihood of tie formation (Contractor et al., 2006). For example, consider the mechanism of preferential attachment. Preferential attachment is the tendency to partner with already popular actors. Thus, one's existing set of ties in the network may influence how attractive they are to others. Unlike the more general social science theories, these mechanisms rely on the network's structure to influence the probability of a tie.

Research examining network formation processes has focused predominately on the mechanisms of homophily, resource dependence, and the variants of social capital (bonding, bridging, and trust). We will explore the application of those theories, and others, more directly in Section 3. A large number of hypotheses, seventy-five in total, did not provide an explicit theory by which the independent variable affected the dependent variable and thus was categorized as NA. These hypotheses were generally supported based on the context or setting of the study. For example, a study by Chen et al. (2019) supported several hypotheses based on the unique features of the Chinese political system. Thus, it is important to note that hypotheses falling under the NA category are not necessarily lacking justification but rather are not directly tied to a specific theory or mechanism.

2.1.2 Theories on Network Effects

For the articles coded as network effects and thus residing on the right side of the Multilevel Network Framework, the prominent mechanisms and theories used to connect network features to network effects are listed in Table 5. That table also describes the theory/mechanism and the number of times it was applied in the literature. For an in-depth discussion of several mechanisms listed in Table 5, see Medina et al. (2021). As with the theories and mechanisms on the network formation side, we again distinguish between general social theories and more network-specific or endogenous factors. We label the endogenous factors as structural arguments in Table 5, as these hypotheses highlight the implications of particular network structures or positions on outcomes.

As with the network formation hypotheses in Table 4, many network effects hypotheses fall into the NA category. As noted above, these are hypotheses for which no explicit theory is provided. For example, Faulk et al. (2016) hypothesize that nonprofit organizations will gain more grants if their board interlocks with foundations. This hypothesis is supported by findings and evidence in the

Table 5 Theories and mechanisms producing network effects

Theoretical category/ mechanism	Description	Number of hypotheses
General social theories		
Collective Action	Benefits from aligned mutual interests and coordinated action.	1
Heterophily	The impact of differences in the attributes and characteristics of the actors in the network; often thought to promote innovation and reduce groupthink.	1
Homophily	The impact of similarity in the attributes and characteristics of the actors in the network; often thought to promote trust, tacit knowledge exchange, and alignment of expectations.	2
Policy Diffusion/Social Influence	The spread of behavior and attitudes via direct network connections or similarity in network position.	10
Resource Dependence	The power dynamics that emerge when actors are reliant on others for critical resources and the implications of those dynamics.	6
Social Capital – Bridging/Brokerage/ Structural Holes	Information and control benefits that accrue to those who broker relations between unconnected actors.	18
Social Capital – Bonding	Benefits of strong ties, commitment, and cooperation associated with densely connected or homogenous groups.	8

Table 5 (cont.)

Theoretical category/ mechanism	Description	Number of hypotheses
Social Capital – Trust	Influence of taking other's interests into account when making decisions on overall network functioning and outcomes.	6
Social Capital – Generic	A generic reference to social capital as a driver of individual or collective performance.	3
Social Exchange	The impact of the similarity or discrepancy in the level and amount of resources exchanged between actors.	3
Network-Specific /Endogenous		
Structural Argument- Centrality	Nodal level – how an actor's position in a network may influence its success. Network level – how the overall centralization of the network may influence collective performance.	45
Structural Argument- Density	The ratio of the number of existing ties to the number of possible ties in a network.	6
Structural Argument- Structural Embeddedness	Overlapping relations; how ties of one type may influence behavior of ties of another type.	8
Structural Argument- Structural Equivalence	Social pressure and similarity in behavior that may result from similarity in network relations.	2
Structural Argument- Transitivity	The impact of structural cohesion and cliques on the development of norms and expectations of behavior.	1

Table 5 (cont.)

Theoretical category/ mechanism	Description	Number of hypotheses
Other/NA		
Multiple	Any hypothesis that relies on more than one theory for support.	5
Other	Any other mechanism not listed above. This group includes hypotheses on entropy theory, cooptation theory, and systems theory.	8
NA	No explicit theory provided; hypothesis supported primarily based on context and setting.	90

general nonprofit management literature rather than grounded in a specific social or organizational theory. Again, the NA category does not mean the hypothesis lacks support or justification; it simply indicates it did not draw upon a specific theory or mechanism.

Structural arguments based on centrality measures were the primary mechanisms by which public administration and policy scholars predict network effects. Centrality has been deemed the "structural importance of a node" and consists of many concepts and measures (Borgatti et al., 2013). Given the prominence of centrality in social network analysis generally, it is perhaps unsurprising to see such an emphasis in our field. Measures used in the literature to capture centrality include betweenness, closeness, eigenvector, power, indegree, and outdegree. The second most common theory used is Social Capital-Bridging/Brokerage/Structural Holes.

Social Capital-Bridging/Brokerage/Structural Holes was also prominent in the network formation literature. While the general category of the theory is the same, the underlying mechanism differs depending on whether it is used to predict network formation or network effects. For instance, on the network formation side, bridging ties are thought to form when individuals seek efficient methods of accessing novel and nonredundant information or in collaborative activities with high asset specificity (Andrew, 2009). On the network effects side, the implications of bridging ties are considered. To the extent that an actor's ties serve as bridges in the network, the potential access to novel information has been linked to innovation and better performance outcomes (Burt, 2004). Several other theories found in Table 4 also appear in Table 5.

How do these different theories and mechanisms relate to the different levels of analysis discussed in Section 1? While several theories operate predominately at one level or along one link, others are used at multiple levels. Sections 3 and 4 will discuss each link in the Multilevel Network Framework and the primary theories and mechanisms used.

3 Network Formation

This section focuses on the left-hand side of the Multilevel Network Framework and explores processes and mechanisms associated with network formation. With networks becoming increasingly essential modes of service delivery and policy making, scholars have naturally developed an interest in understanding the determinants of network formation. From a design perspective, having a better grasp of these determinants helps to facilitate collaboration and collective action. However, understanding network formation or network processes is challenging due to the complexity of networks but also fraught with conceptual confusion as the levels of analysis and units of analysis are often mistaken for one another. We attempt to clarify the different levels of analysis and the mechanisms used to explain network processes with the Multilevel Network Framework. By systematically reviewing the existing network literature and categorizing the hypotheses onto the various links in the Multilevel Network Framework, we provide a unique lens into where scholarly research has focused, the theories and mechanisms used, and future areas of need.

3.1 Mapping Hypotheses to the Multilevel Network Framework

As discussed in Section 1, the level of analysis is based on the research question one is interested in answering. The level of analysis, as established by the dependent variable, determines the number of pertinent observations available for analysis. The level of analysis is consequently connected to different links in the Multilevel Network Framework by considering the explanatory variable. For example, suppose the dependent variable is a dyadic level outcome (say, the presence of a communication tie between two employees at Point C), and the independent variable is a node-level variable (say, an indicator of their level of expertise, at Point B). In that case, the hypothesis is on the micro–micro link (which we label NF2). However, consider a different situation in which the dependent variable is the overall centralization of a service delivery network (a Level 0 variable at Point D), and the explanatory variable is whether there is a legal mandate that funding has to be distributed by a single government agency (Point A). In this situation, the hypothesis linking the mandate to network centralization would fall on the macro–macro link (NF4). Thus, for any given hypothesis, the particular link can be identified by locating the level at which the independent and dependent variables operate. These links also serve as a placeholder for the particular mechanisms that may be a causal factor behind any observed association.

From the 107 network formation articles (72 of which were inferential) identified in our systematic review, we extracted 266 hypotheses and mapped them onto the left-hand side of the Multilevel Network Framework. Figure 5 reveals that twenty-two hypotheses (8.3%) were on the macro–micro link (NF1). This link investigates how network-level factors influence node-level motivations and constraints. Institutionalism scholars have noted that formal and informal institutions establish incentive structures that make certain behaviors more beneficial than others (North, 1991). To maximize their interests, individuals and organizations respond to the incentives provided by institutions and change their behaviors accordingly. For example, the increasingly widespread use of and general acceptance of public–private partnerships (PPPs) may make PPPs a more legitimate or desirable model for providing public services. Such legitimacy serves as a macro-level variable that may shape the motivations and interest of local governments to collaborate with business or nonprofit organizations.

Along the micro–micro link (NF2), we found 206 (77.4%) hypotheses; the most of any of the network formation links. This link focuses on the micro-level dynamics that explain how node-level motivations and constraints influence tie formation and dissolution decisions. For example, scholars may explore what individual factors shape street-level bureaucrats networking behaviors with

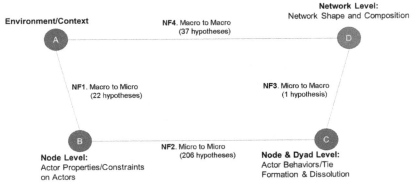

Figure 5 Number of network formation hypotheses on each link

peers. Or, if organizations are the nodes of interest, what organizational attributes drive them to establish collaborative ties for information and resource sharing with other organizations. Understanding the drivers of tie formation is an important area of scholarly research as these ties ultimately shape node and system-level outcomes.

The micro–macro link (NF3) explores how nodal decisions about tie formation and dissolution influence the overall shape and properties of the larger network. Our review suggests that public administration and policy research related to micro–macro relations has been quite limited; only one hypothesis (0.4%) operated along this link. Micro–macro network formation research can explore how individual behaviors produce emergent properties in networks (Baum et al., 2003). Other research may investigate how the strategic removal of a certain node or set of ties can disrupt the function of networks. Such strategies of disruption may be particularly useful in combating terrorist networks or disease spread (Chami et al., 2017; Raab & Milward, 2003).

Finally, we found thirty-seven hypotheses (13.9%) were on the macro–macro link (NF4). This link examines how macro-level factors, such as institutions, policy domain, and the broader organizational context, affect the overall shape and properties of a network. For instance, researchers may study how policy funding or legal mandates produce networks with a particular structure. Such work can provide insight into macro-level variables that explain why service delivery networks are more centralized in some cities or why some municipalities have greater connectivity among employees in different departments.

Next, we will discuss in more detail the types of research questions asked at each of these links and review examples to illustrate how scholars theoretically connect variables operating within and between different levels.

3.1.1 Macro–Micro Hypotheses (NF1)

Macro–micro hypotheses are ones in which macro-level factors (Point A) are used as the predictors and drivers of the constraints and motivations of individual actors in the network (Point B). Here network-level variables (Level 0) influence nodal level constraints and motivations (Level 1). Those constraints and motivations then shape tie formation decisions, which we refer to as dyadic, Level 2 outcomes at Point C. However, it is common for macro–micro hypotheses to skip Point B and focus on how macro-level factors directly influence tie formation in the network. For example, Kapucu and Garayev (2016) examined how nodes' centrality measures differ in emergency management systems that follow different approaches (horizontal vs. vertical). Their reasoning was primarily based on how the two approaches produce different propensities for

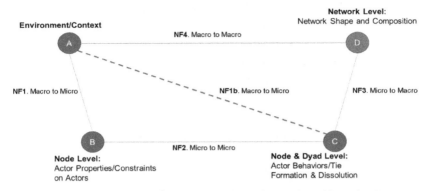

Figure 6 Depicting macro–micro hypotheses that skip point B

forming ties. Instead of exploring directly how nodes' incentives or constraints differed in these two emergency management systems, they provide a structural perspective. Consequently, the nodal level implications of institutional and environmental factors are implicit and not directly hypothesized. As shown in Figure 6, one could consider such hypotheses to fall along a diagonal link from Point A to Point C, a link labeled NF1b. Whether the hypothesis falls along NF1 or NF1b, it is still focused on connecting macro-level environmental and contextual factors to micro-level variables (perceptions and behaviors). Thus, both types of hypotheses are macro–micro, and we consider them together here.

We found thirteen hypotheses that attempt to investigate how macro-level dynamics enable or constrain actors' intentions to form ties with other actors (NF1) and nine hypotheses on the direct implications of macro-level features on tie formation (NF1b). The most widely used theoretical mechanism on this link is collaboration risk/risk hypothesis. The "risk hypothesis" postulates that actors in networks with a widespread risk of defection tend to form bonding structures, while actors in networks with low risk of defection tend to form bridging structures. One example of this mechanism is Berardo and Lubell (2016), who study how bonding and bridging structures vary in settings with different degrees of institutionalization. They hypothesize that network configurations will likely feature weak bonding in weakly institutionalized settings, where policy forums are less formal and the participation of governmental and technically capable actors is marginal. This occurs because the instability of the setting does not allow actors to interact in multiple forums to build strong trust-based relationships. Here the key independent variable is the macro-level condition of the degree of institutionalization of a setting (a Level 0 variable) and how it incentivizes actors against seeking strong relationships (a Level 2, micro-level variable).

Homophily and transitivity/triadic closure are also used as theoretical mechanisms connecting macro and micro phenomena. As an example of attribute-based homophily, Siciliano and Wukich (2017) examine tie formation during disasters. They investigate whether the national capacity for emergency management affects the likelihood of organizational homophily. Their argument is based on macro–micro reasoning: countries with weak emergency management capabilities are unable to establish strong interorganizational relationships during the preparedness stages. Consequently, organizations need to rely on other means, such as similarity in background or locations, to determine potential partnerships when disasters hit. Thus, homophily would be more pronounced in low-capacity nations. The main focus of the explanation is on how the macro-level condition at Point A, national emergency management capacity, constrains or allows organizations to build relationships prior to and during disaster response (Point C). The independent variable is at the macro-level (Level 0), while the dependent variable is at the micro-level (Level 2).

With regard to the number of observations and methods of analysis for macro–micro hypotheses, the dependent variables are micro-level phenomena (Point B or Point C), that operate at the nodal or dyadic level. However, the independent variables are macro-level, such as contextual features or environmental settings in which the network operates (Point A). These macro-level factors consequently only vary at Level 0, the network level. This means that multiple networks are needed for analysis. Of the studies we reviewed, all but one relied on three or fewer networks. Consequently, the research designs are dominated by case studies and comparative case designs.

For example, the Berardo and Lubell (2016) study mentioned above examines the relationship between the institutionalization of governance systems and the resulting bonding and bridging structures. Essentially, they explore how a macro-level factor, the institutionalization of governance systems, affects a micro-level factor, different patterns of tie formation. They use an ERGM, a dyadic level method, to investigate patterns of tie formation. However, to address their key hypothesis of how tie formation varies under governance systems with different degrees of institutionalization, they resort to comparing parameter estimates on the bonding terms in the ERG models. These coefficients are compared across three water governance networks in Argentina, Tampa Bay, and Sacramento that vary in their level of institutionalization. Thus, despite using an ERGM (a dyadic model for Level 2 analyses), the overall design is a small-N comparison of how tie formation tendencies found in the network may vary under different institutional conditions. This is a great example of the complexity associated with developing and testing particular research questions and the data needed to do so.

3.1.2 Micro–Micro Hypotheses (NF2)

Unlike hypotheses on the NF1 and NF1b links that examine macro influences, a large number of studies take a more micro perspective and examine how micro-level attributes (Point B) influence tie formation (Point C). Salient topics studied along the NF2 link include how personal and organizational character-istics affect tie formation. For example, it has been well documented that actors tend to form ties with other actors that share similar attributes, such as gender, race, sector, or geographical location (Borgatti et al., 2013). A primary reason for establishing homophilous ties is that actors tend to equate similarity with trust (Brass, 1995).

The micro–micro level is unquestionably the most common level of study in the current network formation literature, with 206 hypotheses (77.4% of all network formation hypotheses). In terms of network formation, the level of analysis of the dependent variable is dyadic, Level 2, and thus scholars often use ERGM, SAOM, and QAP. The independent variables predicting dyadic behav-ior can range from individual actor attributes (Level 1 variables such as age or location) to dyadic similarity (Level 2 variables such as sharing the same belief or same gender). The four most common theoretical mechanisms used to support micro–micro hypotheses include homophily, social capital-bonding, rational choice, and social capital-trust.

One example of using homophily to explain tie formation is Henry et al. (2011). They study how belief systems affect policy network structure. Using an ERGM, they find that governmental organizations with divergent belief systems are less likely to form collaborative ties. Similarly, Atouba and Shumate (2015) find that international nonprofit organizations working on infectious diseases are more likely to collaborate with nonprofit organizations headquartered in the same global region. This is because they generally confront similar issues, problems, and institutional frameworks.

With regard to applications of social capital-bonding, Huang (2014) exam-ines information-sharing ties established among organizations in an adult men-tal health network. He finds that frequent interactions between organizations provide opportunities for organizations to build a common knowledge base and are thus associated with an increased likelihood of sharing information about service innovations. Nisar and Maroulis (2017) investigate tie formation from the perspective of rational choice and cost–benefit calculations. They find that experienced street-level bureaucrats are more likely to be sought out to discuss work-related issues. They reason that the marginal benefit of discussing work with an experienced colleague is higher than with an inexperienced colleague. In these examples, the operative mechanism starts from the nodal or dyadic characteristics of the actors (sharing the same region or having more experience), and the dependent variable is the formation of ties, a dyadic measure.

Because micro–micro research questions typically center on dyads (Level 2), scholars usually do not need to collect data from a large number of networks for analysis. Instead, data from one whole network often contains a sufficient number of dyads for inferential methods such as QAP or ERGM. For example, Parsons (2020) studies the influence of risk, policy beliefs, and trust on the formation of relational ties. He surveyed forty public and private organizations that work on autism and special education in Virginia and constructed a directed network. Even though the whole network only involves 40 organizations, he has 1,560 dyads to conduct the analysis. The number 1,560 comes from subtracting the self-ties from 40^2 or $40(40-1)$. As shown in Table 3, most of these studies collected data at only a single time point; longitudinal studies of tie formation and network evolution remain rare. Only sixteen of the seventy-two inferential articles that tested micro–micro level hypotheses collected data at more than one time point.

3.1.3 Micro–Macro Hypotheses (NF3)

The NF3 link explores how micro-level dynamics (Point C) may influence the overall shape and composition of networks (Point D). When considering how dyadic decisions can generate network-level properties, it is helpful to distinguish between two types of processes. Snijders and Steglich (2015) differentiate between aggregation effects and proper macro features. Aggregation effects take place when the network-level features are the simple aggregate consequences of micro behavior. For example, take the reciprocity index, which is the proportion of ties in a network that are reciprocated. That macro property of the network can be measured by simply looking at the tie formation behavior of each dyad, and hence, is a direct result of micro-level decisions (Snijders & Steglich, 2015).

In contrast, Snijders and Steglich (2015) offer the example of the average path length as a network feature that cannot be defined by simply aggregating the local dyadic behavior of individual nodes, something they refer to as a proper macro feature. The average path length is defined as the average distance between all possible pairs of nodes. Snijders and Steglich (2015) note that you need a matrix of pairwise geodesic distances (which are the shortest path lengths between each pair of actors in the network), and thus the whole network dataset is needed for the calculation. Thus, the average path length emerges as a macro property of the network rather than being the direct result of micro behavior.

Only one hypothesis focused on the micro–macro link across all network formation articles in public administration and policy. Alpert et al. (2006) conducted a case study of the formation of a regional transportation authority in South Florida. They demonstrate that interpersonal ties between transportation stakeholders (Point C) helped to overcome distrust and hostility between local governments and between government and other sectors, which eventually led to the creation of the South Florida Regional Transportation Authority, a formal regional governance network (Point D). Thus, explanation along this link can explore how dyadic or nodal behaviors affect the overall formation and shape of networks.

3.1.4 Macro–Macro Hypotheses (NF4)

Lastly, we look at hypotheses that focus on macro-level relationships, link NF4 in the framework. At this level, the primary independent variables are macro-level factors that influence network formation (Point A), such as institutional rules, group norms, culture, and environmental conditions. These variables are used to predict a range of network structural characteristics (Point D), such as centralization, density, transitivity, as well as how these structural characteristics change over time.

As an example of macro–macro studies, LeRoux and Carr (2010) investigate why municipal governments signed interlocal agreements with other municipal governments to cooperate on service provision. One of their explanations is centered on the nature of the services: system maintenance services, such as roads, water distribution, and treatment, tend to be provided by highly centralized and dense networks of local governments. The reason is that these services are politically neutral and widely regarded as essential, so it is easier for local governments to collaborate on and reap the benefits of economies of scale. In contrast, residents may have diverse preferences towards lifestyle services, such as parks and recreation, and the provision of these services tend to be more decentralized. Therefore, the service delivery networks that emerge around lifestyle services tend to have low centralization. The explanation is a typical macro–macro one that examines how different institutional settings, here system maintenance versus lifestyle services, impact the overall structure of the service delivery network. As is common with macro–macro explanations, the research does not directly examine the intentions and behaviors of any single local government in the larger network; instead, it focuses on how the nature of the service produces different modes of provision. Hence, the micro-level processes are implicit.

The most popular theoretical mechanism used to study the macro–macro link is resource dependence theory. Lee et al. (2018) examine how policy funding context affects network structure. Policy funding context refers to whether funding for a social service is discretionary or mandated, which affects resource dependence relationships. In a discretionary funding context, the locus of resource dependence usually resides in the legislative and executive processes that allocate the resources. Thus, network structures will feature coalitions formed by resource-seeking organizations in order to engage in legislative advocacy. Since funding is required and stable in a mandated funding environment, forming coalitions to engage in legislative advocacy is only one of several ways to secure resources. Organizations can also try to influence administrative processes. Patterns of tie formation are thus different from the discretionary funding context, resulting in different network structures.

Social capital-bridging is another common mechanism used along the macro–macro link. As one example, Varda (2011) studied network changes after the implementation of the National and Community Service Act that funded AmeriCorps to provide personnel to work in the nonprofit sector. She found that after implementing this new act, communities that previously had higher levels of density and transitivity established more bridging ties within networks and reduced redundancy.

Because the dependent variables on the macro–macro link are network-level properties, such as network structural characteristics, the research questions are at Level 0. Level 0 research questions have a single observation per network. Due to the cost and time required to collect network data, most studies that pose research questions on the NF4 link are single case studies. Among all macro–macro studies, 65 percent used single-case design, and no studies involved more than four cases. The small number of cases limits the variation we can explore and prohibits the use of inferential analysis methods.

4 Network Effects

Section 3 examined the processes and dynamics of network formation. This section moves to the right side of the Multilevel Network Framework and considers the implications, outputs, and outcomes that result from different network compositions and structural properties. Networks are often viewed as a flexible form of organizing that primarily relies on horizontal relationships rather than top-down authority for facilitating information communication and resource coordination. In public administration and policy, networks are often studied as interorganizational arrangements for accomplishing goals that cannot be addressed by a single organization or as a form of governance that differs from hierarchical authorities (Agranoff & McGuire, 2001; Koliba et al., 2011). Public administration and policy also study the consequences of inter-personal networks, such as the relationships among street-level bureaucrats (Nisar & Maroulis, 2017). Evaluating network performance is essential for assessing whether financial, human, and other resources embedded in networks are used efficiently and effectively.

Many factors can influence network effects, including contextual factors (e.g., institutional arrangements and environmental uncertainty) and the functioning and management of networks (Kapucu & Hu, 2020). Our focus is on the role of a network's structural and compositional properties. Understanding the effects of network composition and structure can inform network designs, policy interventions, and network management to achieve collaborative outcomes (Valente, 2012; Whetsell et al., 2020). However, there remains a lack of consensus on the relationship between different network structures and performance (Hu et al., 2022). Furthermore, there is a need to explain the underlying mechanisms linking network properties to their effects. This section reviews network effects research and synthesizes the theoretical mechanisms researchers used to explain network effects across the different links in the Multilevel Network Framework. Before discussing examples of research that operate along each of the links, we begin by addressing how public administration and policy scholars conceptualize and measure network effects.

4.1 Conceptualization and Measurement of Network Effects

Borgatti and Halgin's (2011) categorized network outcomes into two types: choice and success. Network choices are broadly defined as decisions regarding actors' "behaviors, attitudes, beliefs, and (in the case of collective actors like organizations) internal structural characteristics" (Borgatti & Halgin, 2011, p. 8). The similarity in actors' choices has often been studied as one type of network outcome (Borgatti & Halgin, 2011). In public administration and policy, network choice often refers to the decision that an actor makes regarding adopting a new program, management practice or policy; participating in collaboration; or making a significant policy change.

We adapted Borgatti and Halgin's categorizing and differentiated network effects into two categories: choice and performance. Borgatti and Halgin noted that success includes performance rewards at node or whole network levels but did not clearly define what constitutes success. Network performance, rather than success, is more commonly used in public administration and policy. Therefore, we build on Provan and Milward's (2001) work and define network performance as the desired impacts of network relationships and structural properties at the actor, network, and community levels. Existing research has examined how network structures influence the accomplishment of organizational goals and missions and impact organizational legitimacy, commitment, trustworthiness, influence, and reputation (e.g., Koliba et al., 2017; Provan et al., 2009). Client satisfaction with services and programs is also used to measure network performance in education, health, and social services (e.g., Provan & Milward, 1995). In addition, in some domains (e.g., emergency management) where service quality or policy outcomes are difficult to measure, effective communication, decision making, and coordination have been used as proxy performance measures (e.g., Kapucu, 2006). Other studies examine how network relationships and structure impact the stability, function, and growth of networks and the outcomes for the community served by the network[3] (Raab et al., 2015; Wang, 2016; Yi, 2018). In environmental management, it is common to see more context-specific measures of network performance, such as energy consumption and green job growth (e.g., Yi, 2018). Table 6 provides an example of how network scholars analyzed and measured network effects as choice and performance. Of the seventy-four network effects articles included in our analysis, thirty-four examined network choice, and forty studied network performance.

4.2 Mapping Hypotheses to the Multilevel Network Framework

Network effects can occur at the network (Level 0), nodal (Level 1), and dyadic (Level 2) levels. Network effects can be examined by focusing on the four links on the network effects side of the Multilevel Network Framework: macro–micro

---

[3] Provan and Milward (2001) distinguished between three levels of network evaluation. They discussed the organization/participant level, the network level, and the community level. The organization/participant level is the same as our Level 1, or nodal level outcomes. What Provan and Milward refer to as the network level and the community level are both macro outcomes that operate at Level 0. Thus, we consider Provan and Milward's network criteria (such as the range of services provided or the member commitment to the network) and their community-level criteria (such as indicators of client well-being or cost to the community) as operating at the same level. We do so because, for any given network, there is only a single observation of the effectiveness regardless of whether we explore indicators for the network itself or the community it serves. We should also note that different types of networks may not be compatible with each of the effect types discussed by Provan and Milward (2001). For instance, consider the distinctions between purpose-oriented networks and serendipitous ones (Carboni et al., 2019; Kilduff & Tsai, 2003; Nowell & Milward, 2022). Unlike serendipitous networks, purpose-oriented networks are self-referencing, meaning the members consciously affiliate with them. The performance at the network level, as defined by Provan and Milward (2001) to capture the network's range of services, legitimacy, member commitment, and so on, would only be applicable to purpose-oriented networks. It would not make sense to talk about the legitimacy or range of services associated with a friendship or communication network. Performance measures at the participant and community level, however, can be applied to both purpose-oriented and serendipitous networks. For example, consider the serendipitous network of trust-based ties among members of a community or village. At the participant level, individuals in the network may gain benefits, access to resources, and assistance from their connections with others. At the community level, neighborhoods with greater social capital may be more resilient in the face of disasters (Aldrich & Meyer, 2014).

Table 6 Conceptualization, measurements of network effects and their application domains

Network effect type	Possible measures of network effects	Examples in the literature
Choice: Actor decisions, attitudes, beliefs, or behaviors and changes in those decisions, attitudes, beliefs, and behaviors	Adoption of a new program/policy	The number of climate policies a country has adopted in a given time period (Kammerer & Namhata, 2018)
	Participation in cross-boundary organizations, forums, or other collaborations	The number of neighborhood projects in which civic organizations participate (Dekker et al., 2010)
	Job satisfaction; organizational commitment	Employee's emotional attachment and involvement in the organization (Siciliano & Thompson, 2015)
Performance: Desired impacts of network relationships and structures on individual nodes, networks, and communities	Access to resources such as funding and contracts	Organization's ability to secure foundation grants (Faulk et al., 2016)
	Achievement of organizational mission and goals	Perceived advancement of organizational goals in food systems planning networks (Koliba et al., 2017)
	Influence, reputation, legitimacy, and trustworthiness	Perceptions about influence and trustworthiness (Provan et al., 2009)
	Effective communication and decision making	Perception of information flow and technical structure in the organizations (Kapucu, 2006)

Table 6 (cont.)

Network effect type	Possible measures of network effects	Examples in the literature
	Effective coordination of resources; effective collaboration	Member's perceptions of their collaborative's effectiveness in promoting community change, influencing policy, and improving existing services (Nowell, 2009)
	Client satisfaction of services and programs offered	Students' willingness to choose the same program at the same college (Schalk et al., 2009)
	Policy domain-specific performance measures	Renewable energy capacity and green jobs growth (Yi, 2018)

(NE1), micro–micro (NE2), micro–macro (NE3), and macro–macro (NE4). Again, we consider Level 1 and Level 2 variables as micro and Level 0 variables as macro. We mapped out how many hypotheses fall onto each of the four links. As noted in Section 2, we extracted 223 hypotheses. We analyzed each hypothesis, located the level of the independent and dependent variable, identified the mechanism used to explain the network effects, and mapped the hypothesis onto one of the four links. Figures 7a and 7b show the number of hypotheses coded at each link for studies measuring network effects as choice and those measuring network effects as performance.

Among the network performance articles, researchers tend to focus equally on the micro–micro link and macro–macro link. Conversely, among network choice research, researchers develop more hypotheses around the micro–micro link. One reason for this difference in emphasis based on the type of effect is that it may be difficult to observe network-level choices, especially in situations where the network is not mandated or characterized as purpose-oriented. In such instances, more serendipitous networks may not function as a collective (in the sense of making network-wide decisions or coordinating behavior). However, their structure and composition can have collective or system-level implications (Siciliano, Carr et al., 2021).

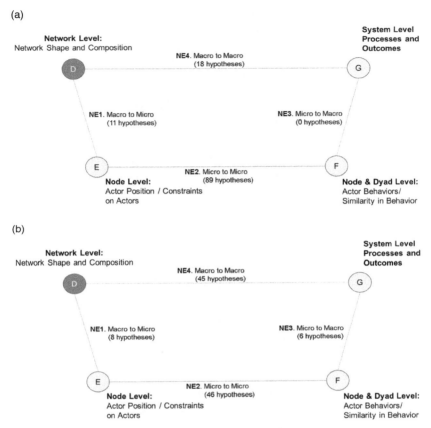

Figure 7 (a) Number of network effects as choice hypotheses on each link; (b) Number of network effects as performance hypotheses on each link

Considering both choice and performance network effects research, nineteen hypotheses were framed at the macro–micro link (NE1). This link explores how network-level factors such as network composition and structural properties lead to node-level network effects. The traditional structural perspective in network research highlights that network structures can establish incentives, place constraints, and influence individual node behavior (Tasselli et al., 2015; Uzzi & Spiro, 2005). Nodes are embedded in networks of relationships; therefore, the aggregate-level patterns of network connections provide the context in which individual nodes act (Tasselli et al., 2015) and thus "facilitate and constrain outcomes of importance" to individual nodes (Kilduff & Brass, 2010, p. 319). The E–I index, discussed at the end of Section 1, demonstrated how the broader shape and connectivity across the network can influence the perceptions and behavior of individual actors. As another example of how network structure can affect individual nodes, consider the density of a network. A dense network can grant members access to information and the ability to monitor other members' behaviors. A dense network can also reduce transaction costs and risky behaviors among network members leading to better collaborative outcomes (Bodin et al., 2017). Thus, the macro properties of networks can have micro-level implications for the members of those networks.

Almost three-fifths of all hypotheses (135) were framed from micro-level factors leading to micro-level effects. The micro–micro link (NE2) explores how node-level factors contribute to node-level or dyad-level effects. With a longstanding research emphasis on the relations between the individual actors in the network (Freeman 2004), the micro–micro link has naturally received much attention in the public administration and policy literature. A node's position and connections within a network (Point E) determine its access to information, knowledge, and resources (Point F) (Borgatti & Cross, 2003), thereby influencing its choices and performance. For example, social capital theory applied at the micro level suggests that dyads' frequent interactions might foster and enhance trust between actors, therefore promoting collaborative outcomes (Borgatti & Cross, 2003). Structural hole theory noted that actors serving as intermediaries between two separate groups of individuals have a strategic advantage via their access to novel and non-redundant information, leading to better performance (Burt, 1992, 2004). Although it is useful to understand how actor attributes or position in the network influence actor behavior or performance, relying only on this research-level limits our understanding of network-level influences.

Only six hypotheses focused on the micro–macro link. The micro–macro link (NE3) allows researchers to understand how micro-level network dynamics (Point F) affect outcomes at the system level (Point G). The micro–macro link is relevant to network research as it examines how system-level outcomes emerge through micro-level behaviors. Thus, interest is in the processes and dynamics through which nodal behaviors and dyadic interactions can scale up to the macro level. For example, when managers are located in central positions in the network, these managers can facilitate information exchange and initiate system-level changes. Bridging a micro–macro gap has been viewed as a critical explanatory step. Many macro-level social events cannot be fully understood through macro-level mechanisms but demand a micro–macro perspective (Aguinis et al., 2011; Coleman, 1990).

Finally, sixty-three hypotheses focused on the relationship between macro-level factors and macro-level effects. The macro–macro link (NE4) studies how network composition and structures (Point D) contribute to system-level changes and outcomes (Point G). For instance, a centralized network can integrate service provision and improve efficiency.[4] "Structure matters" has long been a tenet for network research, and macro–macro-level studies have a long history in network effectiveness research (Provan & Milward, 1995). Networks are also embedded in institutions and policy contexts that can interact with network-level factors and affect the type and quality of effects produced. For example, the resource munificence of a network has been found to affect its performance (Provan & Milward, 1995; Turrini et al., 2010).

4.2.1 Macro–Micro Hypotheses (NE1)

The macro–micro link was one of the least explored. Nineteen hypotheses fall upon the macro–micro link examining how network-level factors (Point D) such as network shape and composition may produce node-level effects such as incentives or constraints on actors (Point E). Like Section 3's discussion of an NF1b link, which makes actor constraints and incentives implicit, macro–micro hypotheses of network effects sometimes follow a similar diagonal path. Here, researchers take a macro-level property of a network and directly hypothesize its implications for actor behavior (Point F). Consequently, actor incentives and constraints are assumed (or not directly measured) and the hypothesized relationship goes directly from Point D to Point F. We consider both types of hypotheses, those that go from Point D to Point E and those that go from Point D to Point F, as macro–micro relationships.

Macro–micro hypotheses relied primarily on structural arguments. Structural arguments focus on the nodal benefits or costs associated with network properties. Several researchers noted that a dense network could give individual nodes easy access to information and resources, facilitate information flow, promote trust-building, affect actors' willingness to adopt innovative behaviors, and enhance performance. For instance, Maroulis (2017) investigated teachers' innovative behaviors in an urban high school. Innovation is considered a behavioral choice of teachers to adopt, create, or try any new classroom activities, and thus as a network effect is classified as network choice. Maroulis (2017) posited that as the network density of a teacher's subgroup increases, so will the teacher's level of innovation. The underlying theoretical mechanism was that higher levels of network closure led to higher levels of trust and

---

[4] Note that while we focus on Points D through G in the Multilevel Network Framework in this section, this does not mean that there are no other factors influencing network performance. For example, Point A features like the context or environment can also shape system-level outcomes at Point G. However, Point A to Point G links can be studied without any specific reference to or measurement of the network connecting the actors in the system. And thus, are not necessarily network-based hypotheses. So while such factors may influence outcomes, they are not the focus of our exploration of network effects.

information-sharing, which eventually contributed to individual innovative behaviors.

For macro-micro hypotheses of network effects, the independent variables are measured at the network level while the dependent variables are at the node level. The large number of node-level observations typically available in these macro–micro studies allows for the use of traditional statistical models, especially multilevel models. For instance, Siciliano (2015b) argued that teachers tend to perform better in a dense network because these connections facilitate rapid information transmission and diffusion. His study collected professional network data from 424 teachers working in 21 public schools. Network density was calculated for each of the 21 schools. Given the nesting of teachers in schools, multi-level models were used to predict the node-level performance of the 424 teachers.

Because it can be difficult to collect data on the large number of networks needed at Level 0, several studies applied comparative case studies to observe the influence of selected network structures on nodes' behaviors. Overall, macro–micro research plays an important role in understanding how variation in network properties can affect the individual actor's behavior and performance. Studies of the macro–micro link suggest that two actors with the same characteristics and skills can have dramatically different performance outcomes based on the broader composition and structure of the network they are embedded in; something over which they have little control (Siciliano, 2015b).

4.2.2 Micro–Micro Hypotheses (NE2)

We found 135 hypotheses operating along the micro–micro link (NE2), the most among the four links. These hypotheses explore how node-level factors such as a node's position in the network can influence its behavior or how connected nodes may adopt similar behaviors. The major theories and structural arguments used along the micro–micro link include centrality, social capital theory, policy diffusion/social influence, resource dependence theory, and homophily theory.

The influence of direct connectedness as measured by degree centrality has been intensively studied in micro–micro network effects research. For example, Arnold et al. (2017) posited that actors with more direct connections would be more likely to adopt High-Volume Hydraulic Fracturing policies. They argue that highly connected actors can obtain useful information regarding the receptivity and concerns of the various economic and social groups relevant to the adoption of the policy. In this regard, having more direct ties with these groups allow actors to adjust their campaigns and maximize support. In a similar study looking at network performance in the field of emergency management,

Marcum et al. (2012) suggested that direct ties allow organizations to exercise a high level of control over their performance via access to and control over information. The underlying explanatory mechanism associated with a node's centrality in the Marcum et al. (2012) and the Arnold et al. (2017) study concerns the information benefits that a unique network position grants the focal node.

However, high direct connectedness might not always lead to better performance. For example, Scott and Thomas (2017) examined how the position of actors within an environmental policy network impacts actors' ability to access financial, human, and technical resources through participation in different collaborative governance regimes (CGRs). The authors suggest that as the number of the CGRs in which an actor participates increases, the actor's level of resources gained through participation decreases due to the transaction costs in terms of time and resource expenditure associated with participating in multiple CGRs. This provides an important caveat to the often-perceived role of centrality. A node's connections and network position do not necessarily lead to better choices or performance, as the costs of maintaining relationships can outweigh the potential benefits. This is likely especially true for nodes with limited resources and suggests the need to consider the specific context when examining network effects.

Social capital – bridging/brokerage/structural holes has also been frequently used by researchers to explain the influence of node-level positions on their behavior or performance. Individuals or organizations taking a broker position are considered to have advantages through their greater access to novel information. For example, in their study of how Finnish employment offices adopted a job search training program, Jokisaari and Vuori (2009) found that offices in brokerage positions received more diverse information and were more likely to adopt new practices. Similarly, when examining a regional environmental governance network, Scott and Thomas (2017) argued that policy actors in brokerage positions would have greater access to resources in the network (however, this claim lacked empirical support).

Policy diffusion/social influence theory has been used to explain how an actor's choice and performance can be influenced by their relationships with other actors in the network. When two actors share the same connections (i.e., having structural equivalence), they are likely to adopt similar policies or behaviors. In addition, an actor's direct connections can also exert influence on their adoption of behaviors and policy. For instance, Cao and Prakash (2011) examined 134 countries' trade policies from 1993 to 2002. They found that when a country's structurally equivalent competitors adopt ISO 9000 (a voluntary quality certification program), then sellers in this country are likely to join as well. In the context of environmental management, Yi et al. (2018) suggest that when provincial leaders in China are appointed to serve another province, the relocation facilitates the diffusion of performance innovations to the new location.

Overall, micro–micro studies focus on how dyadic interactions and nodal position in a network can influence a node's performance or choice. This type of research does not examine how the micro-level dynamics affect the system or network as a whole. Both the dependent and independent variables along link NE2 reside at the micro-level. The analysis level for these studies is typically at Level 1, the nodal level but can also be at Level 2, the dyadic level. Existing studies at Level 1 generally collect a large enough number of observations to conduct traditional statistical analysis. This again is because the outcomes reside at the nodal level, and thus there are N observations available for analysis. For example, Shrestha (2018) examined how an organization's direct connections and relationship strength with others impact its implementation of a water and sanitation program in Nepal. A total of 125 organizations participated in his study; therefore, Shrestha's research had 125 observations available for analysis. Several studies with a Level 2 analysis treat the decision to join a collaboration or the perception of the benefits of joining a collaborative as a network effect. Given the dyadic focus, these studies rely on inferential network analysis methods such as QAP and ERGM. The number of observations at the dyadic level depends on the number of paired relationships observed. For instance, in the study of an environmental policy network, Scott and Thomas 2017) studied the participation of 400 actors in 57 collaborative governance regimes (CGRs) related to ecosystem restoration and recovery in the Puget Sound region of Washington State. Since many organizations participated in more than one CGR, their study included 1,164 organization-CGR dyads in their analysis.

4.2.3 Micro–Macro Hypotheses (NE3)

Among the four links associated with network effects research, micro–macro studies have received the least attention. Only six hypotheses focus on the micro–macro link (NE3). All six hypotheses examined network effects as performance (rather than choice). These effects included system integration and collaborative success. Among the six hypotheses, the most emphasized mechanisms were structural arguments concerning the benefits of centrality and multiplexity in producing system-level outcomes. Thus, many of the studies hypothesized micro–macro relations linking structural variables at Point E to system-level outcomes at Point G.

In terms of centrality, this structural argument concerns the positive effects of a key actor's central position on macro-level consequences. Centrality at the micro-level has been associated with a range of nodal benefits such as an individual's access to resources, control of information, influence, and reputation. Micro–macro studies suggest central positions for key actors in the network, such as managers or policymakers, allow them to impact system-level processes and outcomes (e.g., Bodin et al., 2017; Ofem et al., 2018). For instance, Bodin et al.s' (2017) research on ecosystem-based management in Sweden demonstrates how project leaders' direct connections with other actors can facilitate macro-level network effects. The authors argue that designated project leaders are better able to "mediate, channel information, and coordinate joint activities" (p. 295) when they have significantly more social ties than other actors in the network. Such capacity enables broader information exchange and increases the network's ability for system thinking and integration (p. 295). Thus, the social behavior of particular individuals (a Level 1 micro measure) can produce system-level outcomes (a Level 0 macro measure).

It is worth noting that our coding decisions for several hypotheses was not straightforward. The Bodin et al. (2017) hypothesis provides an instructive example. For instance, one could argue that the centrality of the project leader, as it is in regard to a specific node or set of nodes, is really an attribute of the network and thus should be considered a macro–macro hypothesis. This is a reasonable conclusion to draw. However, we feel that assigning this hypothesis to the micro–macro relation is more accurate and aligned with our reading of Bodin et al.'s (2017) work. We offer three reasons that can provide insight into our decision-making and categorization. First, Bodin et al. (2017) argue that how system-level outcomes arise is through the actions of the individual project managers and their ability to coordinate and manage information flow. It was not about the centralization of the network (a macro property) but rather how the structural position of certain actors facilitates their ability to shape the behavior and knowledge of other actors in the network. In essence, applied to our framework, their argument connects an individual's position in the network (Point E) to their behavior associated with that position (Point F) and eventually to the group's performance (Point G). And while the theory operates through three points, the actual measurement of variables is conducted only at point E (the project manager's social ties) and point G (the system-level outcomes). Second, we considered the methodology used to test the hypothesis. The authors had data on five networks and began by conducting an ERGM for each network to understand the drivers of tie formation. Of relevance to this micro–macro hypothesis was the effect of being a project manager on tie formation. Thus, an actor-attribute variable, in this case a binary indicator of whether the person was a project manager or not, was used to assess how the likelihood of a tie changes when one of the nodes in a dyad switches from a non-project manager to a project manager. This is a micro-level analysis. They then take the coefficient from that term in each of the five cases and compare it to the system-level outcomes for those cases. Hence, the final test of the hypothesis relied on comparative case study methods, but the independent variable itself required micro-level analysis to initially assess. Third, we considered the application of Bodin et al.'s findings to other settings or contexts where one may want to improve the functioning of teams. How would this practical application occur? In this case, it could occur by encouraging the project manager to be more active in forming ties or by providing skills and training to the project manager to improve their sociality and relationships. Such action would constitute an individual, micro-level intervention, not a macro one. Thus, taken together, this line of reasoning would lead us to consider this hypothesis as a micro–macro phenomenon.

Jooho Lee (2013) provides another micro–macro example in the context of local government parking authorities in South Korea. Lee offers a nuanced hypothesis looking at how boundary spanners (individual actors who connect their local government's parking unit to the IT vendor) can shape the overall effectiveness of e-government services. Lee argues that if the boundary spanner connecting the local government parking unit to the IT vendor plays a central role within the local government's knowledge network, then more accurate and up-to-date IT information flows through the network allowing actors to make better informed and timely decisions. As with Bodin et al. (2017), the independent variable is a measure of an individual's or set of individuals' centrality in a network. The dependent variable is the community perception of e-government effectiveness (a network-level outcome).

For micro–macro network effects research, the independent variable is at the micro-level and the dependent variable is at the macro-level. Consequently, the level of analysis is Level 0. Thus, the existing research on the micro–macro link uses only a small number of observations for analysis, ranging from one to five. Comparative case studies and descriptive studies are the most commonly used methods to explore micro–macro relations. For example, both Bodin et al. (2017) and Lee (2013) (discussed earlier) relied on comparative case designs to test their micro–macro hypotheses.

4.2.4 Macro–Macro Hypotheses (NE4)

The number of macro–macro network effects studies ranked second among the four types of network effects research. A total of sixty-three hypotheses examined the linkage between network-level factors and system-level effects, of which forty-five were focused on network performance and eighteen on network choice. The primary theoretical foundations used along the macro–macro link include social capital theory and several structural arguments. The social capital-based hypotheses focus on the impact that network bonding, bridging, and trust have on outcomes at the system level. The structural arguments focused on the benefits of network centrality, density, and structural embeddedness. In addition to social capital and structural arguments, heterophily, collective action, and resource dependence theory were also used as theoretical support for macro–macro hypotheses.

Several studies used social capital-trust to explain how conflicts and distrust among network members negatively affects collaboration. For instance, in his study on community water projects in Nepal, Shrestha (2013) analyzes the relationship between levels of social capital and collaborative success at the macro level in organizing community initiatives. Specifically, the author states that communities with a lower level of internal conflict are more likely to obtain agency funds. Lack of trust among the members translates into lower levels of information sharing about project costs and ultimately affects the design of project proposals and access to agency funds.

Other studies use the bonding mechanism of social capital theory to explain the effects of strong ties on system-level outcomes. For instance, Lee's (2013) study, noted earlier in Section 4.2.3, also tested how strong ties, measured at the network level, between actors in charge of implementing the online parking services and the IT vendor positively impacted the perception of e-government effectiveness. According to Lee (2013), while adopting new technology to implement public services, strong ties promote mutual understanding, reduce uncertainty, and lead to better information and knowledge sharing between the local government and the IT vendor.

Network centralization is a common structural feature posited to influence system-level outcomes. A centralized network structure allows the central node to mobilize and integrate resources and quickly distribute information in the network (Provan & Milward, 1995; Sandström & Carlsson, 2008). For instance, Klaster et al. (2017) analyzed the impact of centralization on goal attainment in the education and employment domain in the Netherlands. They suggested that more centralized networks can reach higher levels of effectiveness due to shorter decision-making and discussion time. Interestingly, highly centralized networks are also shown to lack adaptability in uncertain environments because external shocks on central nodes can cause the breakdown of the entire network (Nowell et al., 2018). The limitations of a centralized network structure have often been observed in the context of emergency management. Consequently, the applicability of certain structural features and mechanisms is likely dependent on the broader policy domain in which the network operates (Siciliano, Carr, et al., 2021).

Another example of network structural features impacting system-level outcomes is connectivity across different and similar types of actors. Heterophily (or heterogeneity) refers to the relationships among actors with different types of knowledge, experience, and backgrounds. Heterophilous ties can provide access to novel and nonredundant information. Conversely, homophily refers to ties among actors of the same type. Nodes with similar characteristics or backgrounds tend to cluster together and develop trust; however, some scholars have argued that maintaining many homophilous ties could be costly and hinder the movement of new and relevant information through a network (Provan et al., 2013). For instance, an example of how heterophily can explain network outcomes can be found in Bodin et al.'s (2017) research. Studying ecological system-based management in Sweden, Bodin and his colleagues suggested that high levels of connectedness among actors from different backgrounds and worldviews positively impacted problem-solving capacity. However, they also noted that heterophily could present potential challenges (e.g., disagreement), making it a non-sufficient condition for collaborative success.

Overall, macro–macro research examines how network properties impact system-level outcomes like collaborative success and system integration. Both the dependent and the independent variables are measured at the macro level. Macro–macro research addresses Level 0 questions, and thus most studies rely on a small number of observations. These studies typically use comparative case designs and QCA for analysis. There are, however, a few studies with a larger number of networks suitable for standard statistical methods. This includes Chapman and Varda (2017), who analyzed 177 different networks, and Nowell (2009) who analyzed 48 networks.

5 Conclusion

To conclude our development and application of the Multilevel Network Framework, we would like to do three things. First, we will briefly review the framework's key elements and explore how it can be used to understand a social system better or to examine a specific mechanism of interest. Second, we will highlight several findings from the Multilevel Network Framework's application to the public administration and policy literature and identify areas for future research. Third, given the limited inquiry of Level 3 questions, we will delve into the potential ways public administration and policy scholars can begin to consider Level 3 questions in their research and the value in doing so.

5.1 Review

We began this Element by explaining the difference between the unit of analysis and the level of analysis in network research. Such a distinction is unnecessary in traditional research but becomes critical when developing and conducting network research. In networks, the units of analysis are the actors that comprise the social system of interest. In other words, the units are types of nodes in the network – humans, organizations, or countries. The level of analysis concerns the structural features and network variables being emphasized in a research question. We highlighted four possible levels of analysis. The network, nodal, dyadic, and cognitive levels were labeled from Level 0 to Level 3. We linked the Level of analysis to the number of observations available for analysis. Given a specific number of nodes in the network, N, the level of analysis being conducted in the study is equal to the exponent (L) in the term N^L that approximates the number of "observations" available for analysis.

The levels of analysis are also related to the amount of interdependency that may exist among the outcomes of interest and how likely one is to violate assumptions of independence underlying many standard statistical models. Thus, given the number of observations available and concerns about interdependency, it is common to see case study methods employed for Level 0 questions (network level), standard statistical methods for Level 1 questions (node level), and ERGMs and SAOMs for Level 2 questions (dyadic level). Methods for appropriately dealing with Level 3 questions are still being developed.

Beyond the distinction between level and unit of analysis, it is necessary to understand that networks can serve as both the dependent and independent variables. Given the different directions of analysis, we separated the study of network phenomena into two types: network formation (where the network is the dependent variable) and network effects (where the network is the independent variable). Combined with micro–macro models from sociology, the level of analysis and direction of analysis provided the foundation for the Multilevel Network Framework, shown here in Figure 8.

Building from Coleman's bathtub model, we treat Level 0 variables as macro-level and Level 1 and Level 2 variables as micro-level. In terms of its overall properties, shape, and composition, the network itself serves as the central node in the framework (Point D). The network formation side examines how institutional, environmental, and contextual factors (Point A) place constraints and incentives on the actors in the network (Point B), which in turn influences their tie formation and dissolution behavior (Point C). Such tie

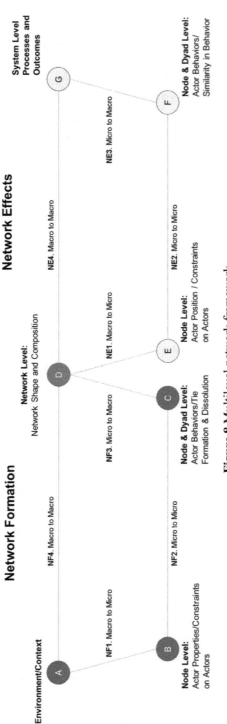

Figure 8 Multilevel network framework

decisions aggregate to form networks with particular properties (Point D). The model also considers the possibility of macro–macro effects.

On the network effects side, we begin with a network having a particular shape and composition (Point D) and consider how such network properties can place constraints on nodes as well as determine the structural position (e.g., betweenness centrality) of a node (Point E). Nodal position and constraints are then linked to behavior (Point F). The behavior of interest can include the output or outcomes of individual nodes or the similarity in behavior or attitudes expressed between two nodes. We then consider the emergence of system-level processes and outcomes (Point G).

As noted in Section 1, the framework serves several roles. It provides a conceptual tool to help us think more deeply about networks and offers a systematic way to categorize research. Thus, one can identify the level and direction of their intended analysis, consider the interdependencies and number of observations available, and explore other research that operates along similar links. At the same time the Multilevel Network Framework provides a scheme to facilitate articulating various social mechanisms and theories that may connect different points in the framework together. It is this latter role that we will explore in more detail here.

Often scholars are interested in a particular social system and want to understand better how the system operates. For instance, the social system could be the informal relations that teachers in a school develop to share knowledge and provide social support for the challenges faced within the classroom. Or it could be the collaborative ties established among workforce development organizations in a region. Given a social system of interest, the Multilevel Network Framework can facilitate the exploration of the various types of questions one can ask and answer to better comprehend how the system operates and evolves.

Suppose a researcher is interested in understanding the social relations and informal ties that connect employees in city government. Thus, the researcher has a specific network in mind; in the sense that they have identified a bounded set of actors whose interactions and outcomes are of interest. Given the setting of a city government and the ties that exist among the employees in the various municipal departments, what types of questions might arise? First, we can place the network at Point D in the Multilevel Network Framework and ask what aspects of the network are of interest? For example, do we care about formal relations, such as co-members of a project team, more informal relations, such as communication, or affective ties, such as friendship?

Then, on the network formation side of the model, we could begin by considering the different factors that operate at Point A, Point B, and Point C.

Perhaps, some city government communication and collaboration networks are highly fragmented, such that ties tend to reside within a given department or agency and therefore the city has very few cross-department ties. What might cause such network shapes to emerge? At Point A, perhaps there are budgeting procedures that create zero-sum funding decisions among departments and thus hinder collaboration. Perhaps there are geographic drivers, such that the departments reside in different buildings and thus prevent personal interactions. At a more micro level, what Point B factors may drive communication? Some of these factors may result from Point A variables, but others may be individual attributes or characteristics. At Point C, there may be endogenous processes that lead to certain tendencies. Perhaps, preferential attachment and transitivity are important self-organizing factors in determining the overall network's shape.

As a researcher looks to better understand and model a given social or governance system, it is useful to begin by exploring the range of research questions and mechanisms that may be operative. Using the Multilevel Network Framework, the researcher can consider which questions are of interest and are answerable given time and budget limits. For instance, while variation at Point A may be an important component in shaping various network structural features, assessing such a Level 0 question requires collecting data on multiple networks. If data on only a single network is currently available, no variation exists at the network level to explore such processes. Thus, for practical reasons, research questions would need to focus on other factors.

Similarly, on the network effects side, scholars can begin to develop a set of possible research questions that operate at different nodes on the right side of the framework. As an exercise in one of our graduate social network analysis classes, we have students identify a social system of interest and then fill out a set of research questions that operate at different levels of analysis. We think scholars, even those with a very focused research question, can benefit from developing a complete theoretical story (or multiple stories) that connects both sides of the Multilevel Network Framework. An example of such an effort was provided in Section 1 (see Figure 3).

One challenge that has been recently noted in the network literature is the inability of research designs to isolate a particular mechanism. Siciliano, Wang et al. (2021) noted that several different potential mechanisms and processes could lead to the same observed network phenomena. The Multilevel Network Framework can help scholars identify possible pathways of influence and identify relevant mechanisms that may be operative. For example, on the network formation side, perhaps you find communication networks in a municipality have a skewed degree distribution, such that there are a few actors with a high degree centrality and many actors with a low degree centrality.

Such network properties can arise through a variety of mechanisms, including (i) efforts to minimize search costs, (ii) actions to facilitate the efficient movement of information, (iii) network self-organization based on preferential attachment, (iv) contexts with high asset specificity, and (v) individual strategic behavior to serve in key bridging roles. Any one of (or combination of) these mechanisms or processes could lead to a network with a skewed degree distribution.

The questions are, how do we know which ones are operating and how much of an impact they are having on a network's shape? Inferential network methods, like ERGMs offer some ability to identify the strength of different mechanisms by placing them in the model simultaneously. However, this requires one to first identify the relevant mechanisms and effectively add them to the model. Once one is explicit about potential processes and mechanisms that give rise to phenomena at a particular point of interest in the framework, those different mechanisms can be considered. The researcher can then determine which processes and mechanisms can be isolated and estimated and which cannot.

Existing methods of analysis at Level 2 (ERGM, SOAM) rely on local structural properties and actor-based decisions. As Robins et al. (2005, p. 895) note: "Network ties emerge, persist, and disappear by virtue of actions made locally at the scale of the individual actors in a network … These local patterns agglomerate to create the global structure." Thus, there is a natural micro–macro connection in Level 2 models. Indeed, the methods by which these models are checked for goodness-of-fit require one to inspect how well networks simulated from the model (which is based only on local configurations and decisions) reproduce the overall macro properties of the network. Thus, providing one with the ability to examine how changes in actor tendencies may have implications on the overall structure of the network.

For instance, take the triad census. The triad census identifies all the possible ways in which three actors can be connected. In a directed network, there are sixteen possible triads. The triad census can facilitate our understanding of how networks with certain properties and shapes emerge from the behavior of the actors within the network (Light & Moody, 2020). As noted by Light and Moody (2020), the local relations among three actors have significant implications for the macro structure of the overall network. They give as an example, the 021 U triad, which indicates a preference for already popular individuals. Such tendencies to form 021 U triads will result in a network that is highly centralized. Using computational and simulation methods based on Level 2 models, researchers can explore how local rules and patterns combine to produce global outcomes and also adjust the strength of local processes to see how the overall shape of the network changes (Robins et al., 2005; Snijders & Steglich, 2015). We find great potential in applying such strategies to public administration and policy networks.

5.2 Findings and Implications

Several key findings emerged in using the Multilevel Network Framework to categorize and explore the extant literature in public administration and policy. First, across both network formation and network effects research, micro–micro hypotheses (NF2 and NE2) account for the majority of all hypotheses tested. While this research has greatly deepened our understanding of the micro factors associated with tie formation and implications of an actor's position on performance, there are limitations to emphasizing micro–micro relations. One obvious limitation is that the micro-level line of research cannot address important network-level questions. For example, what factors influence network sustainability or network performance at the system level? Or what roles do institutional environments play in affecting network structures? Focusing predominantly on the micro–micro link may thus cause scholars to lose sight of interesting and important Level 0 research questions and miss valuable opportunities to further understand how macro factors influence micro behaviors. Such questions are particularly relevant in our field.

Macro-level factors are essential for public administration and policy research as they connect active areas of institutional and governance research (e.g., collaborative governance regimes, collective action challenges) to micro-level collaborative behaviors. Level 0 predictors are fundamental because many of the collaborative settings of interest lack an overarching authority capable of directing the actions of the system's autonomous (or semi-autonomous) actors. Take, for instance, research on collaborative governance regimes and the relationships among a large set of diverse actors interested in improving a watershed. While no single authority exists to guide interactions and behavior, governance strategies through institutional norms, rules, and processes can influence the relationships and outcomes achieved (Ansell & Gash, 2008; Emerson & Nabatchi, 2015; Ostrom, 2009). Thus, understanding how Level 0 macro factors influence tie formation behaviors holds important implications for successfully intervening in networks. For instance, based on previous work, if we seek to create social service delivery networks that are more centralized, what levers or policy tools are available to facilitate a preferential attachment process (Whetsell et al., 2020)? For an overview of potential network intervention strategies in public administration and policy, see Siciliano and Whetsell (2021).

Second, despite data challenges posed by Level 0 research, macro–macro hypotheses were the second most common in the public administration and policy literature. These studies provide critical insight into how macro conditions influence network properties and how those properties affect system-level outcomes. However, studies that explain network formation from a macro-perspective generally ignore the micro-level dynamics. This is potentially problematic as macro–macro-level explanations for social events can be ambiguous because of the possible existence of competing micro-causal relationships. As Coleman (1990, p. 3) states: "A major problem of data adequacy exists in confirmation of theories based on system-level data when the systems are large in size and few in number. There are too many alternative hypotheses which cannot be rejected by the data." In this regard, including micro-level explanations to understand macro-level effects can be insightful (Abell et al., 2014). Of course, it is unfair to ask each study to cover all possible explanatory factors, and as Mayhew (1980) argued, there can be legitimate macro-level explanations. Scholars who oppose methodological individualism believe that there are multiple levels of explanation, and the role of social structure and institutions should not be ignored (Jepperson & Meyer, 2011). As noted above, we find great potential in the application of computational and simulation methods to study these complex multilevel relations.

Third, and as a direct result of the tendency for scholars to focus on a single level of research, either micro–micro or macro–macro, cross-level relationships are rarely explored. The sides of the bathtub creating macro–micro and micro–macro relations (links NF1, NF3, NE1, and NE3), were the least examined links in the framework. We suggest a fruitful avenue for future research would be to develop studies that go through a macro–micro–macro process (from NF1 to NF3 or NE1 to NE3) to explain network formation and network effects. For example, on the network formation side, this causal pathway would attempt to uncover how the dynamic processes underlying the macro-level conditions, such as node intentions and behaviors, give rise to ties and eventually networks with particular shapes. This is precisely the mechanistic detail that Coleman (1990) sought in social science explanation. Coleman (1990, p. 3) argues that "An explanation based on internal analysis of system behavior in terms of actions and orientations of lower-level units is likely to be more stable and general than an explanation which remains at the system level."

A thought experiment may help illustrate how this macro–micro–macro pathway is different from the macro–macro or micro–micro pathway. Suppose a new federal grant program provides resources for local governments in particular regions to collaborate on disaster preparedness and response. A macro–macro-level study would look at the correlation between the awarding of federal grants and the formation of regional emergency management networks. Perhaps looking at the correlation between the presence or absence of grants and network density.

In contrast, a macro–micro–macro study would first explore how the federal grants or legislation affects the intentions or behaviors of local governments: the grants may provide strong incentives for local governments to collaborate or create opportunities or platforms for emergency managers of local governments to get acquainted with one another through meetings or other events. Then scholars would look at how such opportunities or incentives facilitate tie formation or how certain meetings help build personal relationships and trust, leading to collaborative relationships. Addressing the macro–micro–macro processes can help uncover network dynamics that the macro–macro link ignores, and the micro–micro link is unable to test, and thus contributes to a deeper understanding of how a social system operates.

Exploring such multilink pathways through the framework may require the integration of different methods and types of network data. For instance, in the example given above, traditional statistical analyses can be used to test the correlation among the Level 0 variables of grant funding and network density (assuming data in enough regions was collected), while more qualitative work may be needed to understand the individual motivations that lead to the increased formation of network ties. Mixed-method approaches to network dynamics are an exciting avenue for future research. Indeed, as Perry et al. (2018, p. 12) note, "as network research proceeds, the ability to draw in different kinds of network data, from different sources, will likely become an increasingly better match to the complexity of most systems and phenomena."

Considering cross-level influences is also a major point of multilevel theory in the study of organizations, it is necessary to discuss some differences and similarities between multilevel theory and our multilevel network framework. Multilevel theory shares a similar concern that research on organizations has traditionally focused on one single level (Klein & Kozlowski, 2000), even though organizations are multilevel systems. For example, organizational behavior scholars may only focus on individual attitudes or attributes and ignore macro-level factors such as organizational performance; in contrast, macro scholars tend to explain organizational performance based on organizational attributes and ignore individual factors. Multilevel theory recognizes the importance of considering cross-level influences in explaining organizational phenomena and aims to develop comprehensive explanations that include concepts from multiple levels of analysis (Klein & Kozlowski 2000). For instance, to study institutions, which is a macro-level concept, it is important to consider how individual perceptions and judgment are the foundation for institutions to obtain legitimacy (Bitektine & Haack, 2015). In this context, the multiple levels of analysis are in fact, multiple units of analysis, such as individuals and organizations or individuals and institutions. Such terminology parallels research on hierarchical and multilevel models (Hox, 2010).

Networks are also multilevel systems. A single network comprised of a single unit type, say organizations, consists of multiple levels of analysis (nodal, dyadic, network). The terminology can thus become quite confusing when network scholars and organizational scholars use macro–micro and levels of analysis to refer to different things. In networks, the multiple levels are about the different features of the network that can be explored, rather than different units. Consequently, researchers need to be cautious when describing the phenomena of interest, the relevant levels, and the interdependencies among those levels.

The network literature and the multilevel theory and modeling literature have recently begun to merge. There are two general streams of research. The first, referred to as *multilevel network analysis,* concerns the application of network modeling to multiple independent groups (Lazega & Snijders, 2015). The term multilevel is used here to draw explicit connections to traditional multilevel modeling approaches. For instance, one may gather data on service delivery networks in several dozen cities. Each city is seen as an independent network and the data are combined into a single model, such as an ERGM, which permits the parameters to vary for each city. Such approaches allow for greater generalization of the findings compared to research, which historically, has tended to focus only on a single network. Koskinen and Snijders (2022) have developed strategies for longitudinal multilevel analysis using stochastic actor-oriented models.

The second stream of research is referred to as the *analysis of multilevel networks* (Lazega & Snijders, 2015). Here, rather than collecting data on a number of independent networks, each comprised of the same type of node or unit, the data now consists of different types of nodes (Wang et al., 2013, 2016). Modeling strategies are focused on understanding the structure and dependencies within and between the different node types. Figure 9 provides an example of such a system. The term multilevel in this context thus refers to the fact that there are macro and micro node types. For instance, Zappa and Lomi (2015) use multilevel exponential random graph models (MERGMs) to explore how informal communication ties among managers shape and are shaped by the formal structure connecting the organization's subunits. Their work demonstrates a "feasible analytic strategy to represent multilevel mechanisms of network tie formation" (p. 562).

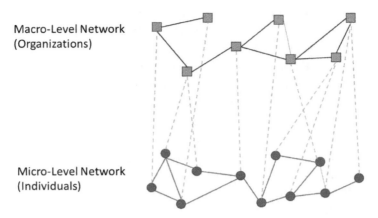

Macro-Level Network
(Organizations)

Micro-Level Network
(Individuals)

Figure 9 A representation of a multilevel network

Fourth, the systematic review revealed that a number of studies skip certain nodes in the framework or make such nodes implicit in the causal process under study. For instance, a study may discuss how macro-level conditions directly affect tie formation without detailed theorizing about how the macro-condition first affects node perceptions, incentives, or constraints. This approach was identified by the diagonal micro–macro link (as shown in Figure 6) connecting contextual variables (Point A) to actor social behavior (Point C). Wang et al. (2021) provide an example of this link. They investigate how urbanism (defined as large, dense, diverse places with the presence of diverse businesses and other institutions) affects social ties. They hypothesized that urbanism might affect both the number of ties that people form with others and the strength of these ties. With big data from a mobile phone company in Spain, they found support for their hypothesis. However, the study (due to the nature of its data) was unable to measure how individuals' intentions or behaviors change in an urban society, which in turn changes how they maintain relationships with others. While their work provides important insight into network dynamics, clearer micro-level theorizing and testing of the changes in individuals' intentions or behaviors could deepen our understanding of the mechanisms through which urbanism affects social ties. Again, we are not arguing that all points of the framework need to be accounted for in any study (nor are we critiquing the studies that make certain points implicit). However, it is useful to know what is emphasized and what is not and the potential implications of those decisions. At the very least, such knowledge can identify areas for future research.

Fifth, the same theory and mechanisms have been used at different levels and directions of analysis. For instance, social capital theory is one of the primary theories that researchers frequently use to explain why certain network structures or nodal positions contribute to network choice and performance. There is a need to clarify how social capital is operationalized (Payne et al., 2011). Social capital can refer to the benefits and resources that actors receive through their connections with others (micro-level operationalization) and can also refer to norms and trust that facilitate collective outcomes (macro-level operationalization) (Burt, 1992; Putnam, 1995).

More profoundly, the underlying model by which a theory or concept operates can vary considerably. Borgatti and Lopez-Kidwell (2011) discuss how variation in actor performance can result through two different models associated with social capital. In what they refer to as a network flow model of social capital, they contend that "nodes acquire ideas, resources, and opportunities through their ties" (p. 48). Thus, an actor may achieve better outcomes than another because they are better situated to obtain whatever valuable resources are flowing through the network. In that regard, actors capitalize on their ties to other nodes to increase their own human capital. Alternatively, Borgatti and Lopez-Kidwell (2011) suggest another model of social capital, the network architecture model. Here, node or group success is based on one's ability to "coordinate, or 'virtually agglomerate' multiple nodes in order to bring all of their resources to bear in a coordinated fashion (and avoid being divided and conquered)" (p. 48). Thus, actors may perform better because they can effectively coordinate the behavior and actions of others. Research in public administration and policy is often unclear about which model is being posited when suggesting the benefits of social capital.

Such distinctions of where and how benefits arise to nodes in the network are critical for public administration and policy scholars. If we want to argue that centrality matters or that density matters, we need to be specific about the underlying rationale as to why. Is it because of what is flowing through the network and the resources actors acquire, or instead, is it about the ability to coordinate the actions of other network members? These are two very distinct models. Thus, as Borgatti and Lopez-Kidwell (2011) argue, even basic concepts like centrality are not simply representations of a theoretical concept but also embody a model of how the social system operates.

5.3 Level 3 Research

Finally, we want to discuss the lack of Level 3 research in our field and highlight the value such a research agenda can bring. No study in our systematic review collected or analyzed Level 3 data. Level 3 data, as noted in Section 1, concerns three-dimensional network structures representing each individual actor's perception of the entire network (Krackhardt, 1987). This type of data are typically referred to as cognitive social structures (CSS). Unlike traditional network data collection methods, which often ask each actor to comment on their direct ties with others, CSS data require each actor to provide their assessment of all possible ties in the network. Thus, for a directed network of 10 nodes, each individual actor would provide their perception of the ties between all pairs of actors, in this case, $N(N - 1)$ or 90 ties. Combining each of the 10 actor's perceptions of the network produces a $10 \times 10 \times 10$ array. Excluding self-ties on the diagonal, a researcher would have approximately N^3 observations, hence Level 3 data.

Introduced in 1987 (Krackhardt, 1987), the cognitive social structures frame was an attempt to recognize that actors' perceptions of the network they were embedded in were an important aspect of structures that, up until then, were simply considered "errors." Indeed, a set of studies conducted by Bernard & Killworth (Bernard & Killworth, 1977; Bernard et al., 1982; Killworth & Bernard, 1976) showed that people consistently misperceived their own behavioral interaction patterns, let alone being able to correctly record ties among others in the network. Drawing on W. I. Thomas' famous dictum "If men define situations as real, they are real in their consequences," Krackhardt (1987) argued that these Bernard-Kilworth results could be interpreted another way and that this disjuncture between behavior and perceptions provided an opportunity to explore perceptions in their own right.

Since then, there have been hundreds of studies of cognitive social structures (see Brands, 2013 for a review). They have been applied to many different fields, from psychology, social psychology, organizational behavior, political science, sociology to statistics. One can systematically organize these studies into three categories of research questions: (1) questions of accuracy, (2) questions of essence, and (3) questions of function.

Questions of accuracy ask to what extent do people perceive the "true" network accurately? This was one of the first questions to emerge from this literature, and it remains to this day a popular research angle. For example, Krackhardt (1990) demonstrated that having an accurate picture of the network is related to how much power is attributed to that person.

One of the challenging sub-problems with exploring this question of accuracy, though, is that to do so presumes we have a good understanding or measure of "truth." But, when it comes to actual relationships, such a common understanding of truth can be difficult to pin down. Krackhardt proposed that there are two ways to approach this question of truth: (1) a "locally aggregated structure" (LAS) and (2) a Consensus Structure (CS). An LAS definition assumes the two people involved in a tie are in the best position to evaluate whether that tie exists or not. For example, two people are friends if they consider each other friends.

This definition has been the most commonly used measure of truth (i.e., the true network) in research on accuracy. This definition of truth has been used to study the effects of accuracy (Krackhardt, 1990), its causes (Krackhardt & Kilduff, 1999), and imputation methods for missing network data (Siciliano et al., 2012).

This dominant view of "truth", however, has not gone unchallenged. Butts (2003), in a very clever reanalysis of earlier CSS data, forcefully argued that the evidence is in favor of considering "truth" of a network as measured by the consensus among all the actors participating in the network. He draws on the cultural consensus model of anthropology to amend the original straight voting method proposed in Krackhardt's original consensus formulation. Further, he argues that the consensus among actors signifies a cultural truth, representing social facts that override any individual aberrant and random assessment.

The second category of questions, questions of essence, takes the W. I. Thomas dictum seriously. This line of research explores whether the perceptions of the networks in and of themselves have consequences (or causes), independent of whether they reflect any objective reality. An excellent example of this work is the recent study by Iorio (2022). Through a set of experiments and field studies, he demonstrated how trust is attributed to those who are perceived by others as embedded in a dense network of friends. At the same time, he reaffirmed how having lots of structural holes in the actual network – the opposite of being embedded – leads to more power and influence. Thus, the best of all worlds, the secret to being both powerful and trusted, he found, is to be (mis)perceived as being surrounded by a dense network yet in fact be tied to many who are not so embedded. That is, perceptions carry their own consequences, independent of their attachment to reality.

The third category, questions of function, digs the deepest into the Level 3 data. Such questions suggest that the organizational system functions specifically in response to the minute most detailed level of these perceptions. That is, it asks the direct question, how does person k relate to person i because of k's perception of i's relationship to person j? The answer to this question would be different for every $[i,j,k]$ triple; no aggregation would be needed to pursue it.

One of the best examples of this line of work is Lazega's classic study of law firm partners. He asked each partner in the firm a hypothetical question about each other partner (Lazega, 2001, p. 207):

> Here is a list of all partners in the firm. I would like you to imagine that you are the managing partner. You notice that X is having personal problems. It could be anything, from alcohol to depression, or divorce. But it has repercussions on his or her performance. As a managing partner, it is your job to do something about it. You are looking for colleagues of his or hers among the other partners of the firm to intercede on a discreet and confidential basis, to

go and talk to him or her, see what's going on, what the firm can do to help, and give unsolicited advice. You don't want to do this yourself because you want to keep it informal, and your position would be in the way. My question is: who are the persons among all the other partners whom you would ask to approach X, and why would you delegate this task to them?

Note that the choice the respondent makes in this hypothetical is who the respondent thinks would be effective at influencing and helpful to Partner X. That is, this is a Level 3 question that directly reveals how individuals see the relevant influence/trust network in a way that would directly affect how they would deal with an organizational or personnel issue. This understanding and perception of the network itself have direct implications for the choices that people make, in how they behave with each other, in their organizational life (Lazega & Krackhardt, 2000).

Each of these three categories (accuracy, essence, and function) of CSS research has yet to be explored in public administration and policy. While a full exploration of applications is beyond the scope of this Element, we offer one example to motivate future work. A prominent theory for understanding collaboration structures is the risk hypothesis. The risk hypothesis argues "that actors seek bridging relationships (well-connected, popular partners that maximize their access to information) when cooperation involves low risks, but seek bonding relationships (transitive, reciprocal relationships that maximize credibility) when risks of defection increase" (Berardo & Scholz, 2010, p. 632). Thus, actors actively seek partners with particular ties or structural positions in order to mitigate uncertainty and risk. Actors are, therefore, strategically forming ties based on the benefits the resulting structure will bring. The notion of strategic tie formation is important, and CSS offers an opportunity to investigate the ability of actors to accurately perceive the structures that would emerge from a series of tie formation decisions. For example, do actors have an accurate perception of whom their potential partners are already connected with? In other words, are they aware that a tie with actor A would form a bonding structure while a tie with actor B would form a bridging structure? Such knowledge requires accurate perceptions of the relationships other members in the network have with each other. Future research could examine the cognitive accuracy of actors and assess how accuracy influences their ability to mitigate risk through structural mechanisms.

5.4 Final Thought

As an applied field, public administration, management, and policy scholars are interested in networks not simply because they are a critical part of our society but also with the intention to use networks to improve human and social conditions. Ultimately, our field needs to view networks as a policy and management tool for which we can conceptualize and enact network interventions (Valente, 2012). Consequently, we need to understand the mechanisms that operate in and on networks. We need careful articulation of relevant theory. As Frank and Xu (2020, p. 289) argue, the core challenge in science is being able to differentiate among competing explanations and to "discern among these explanations we need good theory (Wellman & Berkowitz, 1988), good data, and a model that can support scientific discourse about the mechanisms of an effect." This Element aimed to facilitate our ability to test theory, identify data needs, and select appropriate analytic tools.

Given the range, depth, and quality of the empirical work we reviewed, we are optimistic about the future of network scholarship in our field. Network theories and methods are critical tools for studying management and policy problems that cross jurisdictional and functional boundaries. Moreover, governance of public goods and collective action challenges require collaboration and the integration of ideas and resources from multiple actors and sectors. The Multilevel Network Framework provides a conceptual, research, and diagnostic tool for scholars and practitioners interested in exploring network processes, measures, and mechanisms. Overall, we hope this Element serves as a valuable resource for thinking about, critiquing, and developing network research and theory.

References

Abell, P., Felin, T., & Foss, N. J. (2014). Microfoundations of Social Theory. A Response to Jepperson and Meyer. *Sociologica*, *8*(2), 1–12.

adams, J. (2020). *Gathering Social Network Data*. Los Angeles, CA: SAGE.

Agranoff, R., & McGuire, M. (2001). Big Questions in Public Network Management Research. *Journal of Public Administration Research and Theory*, *11*(3), 295–326.

Aguinis, H., Boyd, B. K., Pierce, C. A., & Short, J. C. (2011). Walking New Avenues in Management Research Methods and Theories: Bridging Micro and Macro Domains. *Journal of Management*, *37*(2), 395–403. http://doi.org/10.1177/0149206310382456

Akkerman, A., Torenvlied, R., & Schalk, J. (2012). Two-level Effects of Interorganizational Network Collaboration on Graduate Satisfaction: A Comparison of Five Intercollege Networks in Dutch Higher Education. *The American Review of Public Administration*, *42*(6), 654–677.

Aldrich, D. P. & Meyer, M. A. (2015). Social capital and community resilience. *American Behavioral Scientist*, *59*(2), 254–269.

Alpert, L., Gainsborough, J. F., & Wallis, A. (2006). Building the Capacity to Act Regionally: Formationof the Regional Transportation Authority in South Florida. *Urban Affairs Review*, *42*(2), 143–168. http://doi.org/10.1177/1078087406291591

Anderson, C. J., Wasserman, S., & Crouch, B. (1999). A p* Primer: Logit Models for Social Networks. *Social Networks*, *21*(1), 37–66.

Andrew, S. A. (2009). Regional Integration Through Contracting Networks: An Empirical Analysis of Institutional Collection Action Framework. *Urban Affairs Review*, *44*(3), 378–402. http://doi.org/10.1177/1078087408323941

Ansell, C., & Gash, A. (2008). Collaborative Governance in Theory and Practice. *Journal of Public Administration Research and Theory*, *18*(4), 543–571. http://doi.org/10.1093/jopart/mum032

Arnold, G., Nguyen Long, L. A., & Gottlieb, M. (2017). Social Networks and Policy Entrepreneurship: How Relationships Shape Municipal Decision Making about High-Volume Hydraulic Fracturing. *Policy Studies Journal*, *45*(3), 414–441. https://doi.org/10.1111/psj.12175

Atouba, Y. C., & Shumate, M. (2015). International Nonprofit Collaboration: Examining the Role of Homophily. *Nonprofit and Voluntary Sector Quarterly*, *44*(3), 587–608. http://doi.org/10.1177/0899764014524991

Baum, J. A. C., Shipilov, A. V., & Rowley, T. J. (2003). Where do small worlds come from? *Industrial and Corporate Change, 12*(4), 697–725. http://doi.org/10.1093/icc/12.4.697

Berardo, R., & Lubell, M. (2016). Understanding What Shapes a Polycentric Governance System. *Public Administration Review, 76*(5), 738–751. http://doi.org/10.1111/puar.12532

Berardo, R., & Scholz, J. T. (2010). Self-Organizing Policy Networks: Risk, Partner Selection, and Cooperation in Estuaries. *American Journal of Political Science, 54*(3), 632–649. http://doi.org/10.1111/j.1540-5907.2010.00451.x

Berardo, R., Fischer, M., & Hamilton, M. (2020). Collaborative Governance and the Challenges of Network-Based Research. *The American Review of Public Administration, 50*(8), 898–913. http://doi.org/10.1177/0275074020927792

Bernard, H. R., & Killworth, P. D. (1977). Informant Accuracy in Social Network Data II. *Human Communication Research, 4*(1), 3–18.

Bernard, H. R., Killworth, P. D., & Sailer, L. (1982). Informant Accuracy in Social-Network Data V. An Experimental Attempt to Predict Actual Communication from Recall Data. *Social Science Research, 11*(1), 30–66.

Bernick, E., & Krueger, S. (2010). An Assessment of Journal Quality in Public Administration. *International Journal of Public Administration, 33*(2), 98–106. http://doi.org/10.1080/01900690903188891

Bitektine, A., & Haack, P. (2015). The "Macro" and the "Micro" of Legitimacy: Toward a Multilevel Theory of the Legitimacy Process. *Academy of Management Review, 40*(1), 49–75. http://doi.org/10.5465/amr.2013.0318

Bodin, Ö., Sandström, A., & Crona, B. (2017). Collaborative Networks for Effective Ecosystem-Based Management: A Set of Working Hypotheses. *Policy Studies Journal, 45*(2), 289–314. http://doi.org/10.1111/psj.12146

Borgatti, S. P., & Cross, R. (2003). A Relational View of Information Seeking and Learning in Social Networks. *Management Science, 49*(4), 432–445. http://doi.org/10.1287/mnsc.49.4.432.14428

Borgatti, S. P., Everett, M. G., & Johnson, J. C. (2013). *Analyzing Social Networks*. Thousand Oaks, CA: SAGE.

Borgatti, S. P., & Halgin, D. S. (2011). On Network Theory. *Organization Science, 22*(5), 1168–1181. http://doi.org/10.1287/orsc.1100.0641

Borgatti, S. P., & Lopez-Kidwell, V. (2011). Network Theory. In J. Scott & P. J. Carrington (Eds.), *The SAGE Handbook of Social Network Analysis* (pp. 40–54). Thousand Oaks, CA: SAGE.

Brands, R. A. (2013). Cognitive Social Structures in Social Network Research: A Review. *Journal of Organizational Behavior, 34*(S1), S82-S103. http://doi.org/https://doi.org/10.1002/job.1890

Brass, D. J. (1995). A Social Network Perspective on Human Resources Management. *Research in Personnel and Human Resources Management, 13* (1), 39–79.

Bunger, A. C. (2013). Administrative Coordination in Nonprofit Human Service Delivery Networks: The Role of Competition and Trust. *Nonprofit and Voluntary Sector Quarterly, 42*(6), 1155–1175. http://doi.org/10.1177/0899764012451369

Burt, R. S. (1992). *Structural Holes: The Social Structure of Competition.* Cambridge, MA: Harvard University Press.

Burt, R. S. (2004). Structural Holes and Good Ideas. *American Journal of Sociology, 110*(2), 349–399. http://doi.org/10.1086/421787

Butts, C. T. (2003). Network Inference, Error, and Informant (in)accuracy: A Bayesian Approach. *Social Networks, 25*(2), 103–140.

Butts, C. T. (2008). A Relational Event Framework for Social Action. *Sociological Methodology, 38*(1), 155–200. https://doi.org/10.1111/j.1467-9531.2008.00203.x

Cao, X., & Prakash, A. (2011). Growing Exports by Signaling Product Quality: Trade Competition and the Cross-National Diffusion of Iso 9000 Quality Standards. *Journal of Policy Analysis and Management, 30*(1), 111–135. https://doi.org/10.1002/pam.20546

Carboni, J. L., Saz-Carranza, A., Raab, J., & Isett, K. R. (2019). Taking Dimensions of Purpose-Oriented Networks Seriously. *Perspectives on Public Management and Governance, 2*(3), 187–201. http://doi.org/10.1093/ppmgov/gvz011

Chami, G. F., Ahnert, S. E., Kabatereine, N. B., & Tukahebwa, E. M. (2017). Social Network Fragmentation and Community Health. *Proceedings of the National Academy of Sciences, 114*(36), E7425-E7431. http://doi.org/10.1073/pnas.1700166114

Chapman, C. L., & Varda, D. M. (2017). Nonprofit Resource Contribution and Mission Alignment in Interorganizational, Cross-Sector Public Health Networks. *Nonprofit and Voluntary Sector Quarterly, 46*(5), 1052–1072. http://doi.org/10.1177/0899764017713875

Chen, B., Ma, J., Feiock, R., & Suo, L. (2019). Factors Influencing Participation in Bilateral Interprovincial Agreements: Evidence from China's Pan Pearl River Delta. *Urban Affairs Review, 55*(3), 923–949. http://doi.org/10.1177/1078087418825002

Coleman, J. S. (1990). *Foundations of Social Theory.* Cambridge, MA: Belknap Press.

Considine, M., Lewis, J. M., & Alexander, D. (2009). *Networks, Innovation and Public Policy: Politicians, Bureaucrats and the Pathways to Change inside Government.* Houndsmills: Palgrave Macmillan.

Contractor, N. S., Wasserman, S., & Faust, K. (2006). Testing Multitheoretical, Multilevel Hypotheses About Organizational Networks: An Analytic Framework and Empirical Example. *Academy of Management Review, 31* (3), 681–703.

Cranmer, S. J., Desmarais, B. A., & Morgan, J. W. (2021). *Inferential Network Analysis.* Cambridge: Cambridge University Press.

Crespi, M. (2020). *Examining Physician Referral Networks and Hospital Performance.* (Doctoral Thesis). Pittsburgh: Carnegie Mellon University.

Dekker, D., Krackhardt, D., & Snijders, T., A. B. (2007). Sensitivity of MRQAP Tests to Collinearity and Autocorrelation Conditions. *Psychometrika, 72*(4), 563–581.

Dekker, K., Völker, B., Lelieveldt, H., & Torenvlied, R. (2010). Civic Engagement in Urban Neighborhoods: Does the Network of Civic Organizations Influence Participation in Neighborhood Projects? *Journal of Urban Affairs, 32*(5), 609–632. https://doi.org/10.1111/j.1467-9906.2010.00524.x

Deutsch, M. (1949). A Theory of Co-operation and Competition. *Human Relations, 2*(2), 129–152. http://doi.org/10.1177/001872674900200204

Doreian, P., Teuter, K., & Wang, C.-H. (1984). Network Autocorrelation Models. *Sociological Methods & Research, 13*(2), 155–200. http://doi.org/10.1177/0049124184013002001

Edmondson, A. (1999). Psychological Safety and Learning Behavior in Work Teams. *Administrative Science Quarterly, 44*(2), 350–383. http://doi.org/10.2307/2666999

Emerson, K., & Nabatchi, T. (2015). *Collaborative Governance Regimes.* Washington, DC: Georgetown University Press.

Faulk, L., Willems, J., McGinnis Johnson, J., & Stewart, A. J. (2016). Network Connections and Competitively Awarded Funding: The Impacts of Board Network Structures and Status Interlocks on Nonprofit Organizations' Foundation Grant Acquisition. *Public Management Review, 18*(10), 1425–1455. http://doi.org/10.1080/14719037.2015.1112421

Forrester, J. P., & Watson, S. S. (1994). An Assessment of Public Administration Journals: The Perspective of Editors and Editorial Board Members. *Public Administration Review, 54*(5), 474–482. http://doi.org/10.2307/976433

Frank, K. A., & Xu, R. (2020). Causal Inference for Social Network Analysis. In R. Light & J. Moody (Eds.), *The Oxford Handbook of Social Networks* (pp. 288–310). New York: Oxford University Press.

Freeman, Linton (2004). The Development of Social Network Analysis: A Study in the Sociology of Science. Vancouver: Empirical Press.

Friedkin, N. E., & Johnsen, E. C. (2011). *Social Influence Network Theory: A Sociological Examination of Small Group Dynamics.* Cambridge: Cambridge University Press.

Hambrick Jr., R. S., & Rog, D. J. (2000). The Pursuit of Coordination: The Organizational Dimension in the Response to Homelessness. *Policy Studies Journal, 28*(2), 353–364. https://doi.org/10.1111/j.1541-0072.2000.tb02035.x

Henry, A. D., Lubell, M., & McCoy, M. (2011). Belief Systems and Social Capital as Drivers of Policy Network Structure: The Case of California Regional Planning. *Journal of Public Administration Research and Theory, 21*(3), 419–444. http://doi.org/10.1093/jopart/muq042

Hox, J. J. (2010). *Multilevel Analysis : Techniques and Applications* (2nd ed.). New York: Routledge.

Hu, Q., Medina, A., Siciliano, M. D., & Wang, W. (2022). Network Structures and Network Effects Across Management and Policy Contexts: A Systematic Review. *American Society for Public Administration Annual Conference,* 1–20. https://doi.org/10.1111/padm.12835

Huang, K. (2014). Knowledge Sharing in a Third-Party-Governed Health and Human Services Network. *Public Administration Review, 74*(5), 587–598. https://doi.org/10.1111/puar.12222

Hugg, V. G. (2020). Public Service-Function Types and Interlocal Agreement Network Structure: A Longitudinal Study of Iowa. *Urban Affairs Review, 56* (4), 1293–1315. https://doi.org/10.1177/1078087419843189

Iorio, A. (2022). Brokers in Disguise: The Joint Effect of Actual Brokerage and Socially Perceived Brokerage on Network Advantage. *Administrative Science Quarterly.* https://doi.org/10.1177/00018392221092242

Jepperson, R., & Meyer, J. W. (2011). Multiple Levels of Analysis and the Limitations of Methodological Individualisms. *Sociological Theory, 29*(1), 54–73. https://doi.org/10.1111/j.1467-9558.2010.01387.x

Jokisaari, M., & Vuori, J. (2009). The Role of Reference Groups and Network Position in the Timing of Employment Service Adoption. *Journal of Public Administration Research and Theory, 20*(1), 137–156. https://doi.org/10.1093/jopart/mun039

Kammerer, M., & Namhata, C. (2018). What Drives the Adoption of Climate Change Mitigation Policy? A Dynamic Network Approach to Policy Diffusion. *Policy Sciences, 51*(4), 477–513. https://doi.org/10.1007/s11077-018-9332-6

Kapucu, N. (2006). Interagency Communication Networks During Emergencies: Boundary Spanners in Multiagency Coordination. *The American Review of Public Administration, 36*(2), 207–225. https://doi.org/10.1177/0275074005280605

Kapucu, N., & Garayev, V. (2016). Structure and Network Performance: Horizontal and Vertical Networks in Emergency Management. *Administration & Society, 48* (8), 931–961. https://doi.org/10.1177/0095399714541270

Kapucu, N., & Hu, Q. (2020). *Network Governance: Theories, Frameworks, and Applications*. New York: Routledge.

Kapucu, N., Hu, Q., & Khosa, S. (2017). The State of Network Research in Public Administration. *Administration & Society*, *49*(8), 1087–1120. https://doi.org/10.1177/0095399714555752

Kilduff, M., & Brass, D. J. (2010). Organizational Social Network Research: Core Ideas and Key Debates. *The Academy of Management Annals*, *4*(1), 317–357. https://doi.org/10.1080/19416520.2010.494827

Kilduff, M., & Krackhardt, D. (1994). Bringing the Individual Back in: A Structural Analysis of the Internal Market for Reputation in Organizations. *Academy of Management Journal*, *37*(1), 87–108. https://doi.org/10.2307/256771

Kilduff, M., & Krackhardt, D. (2008). *Interpersonal Networks in Organizations: Cognition, Personality, Dynamics, and Culture*. Cambridge: Cambridge University Press.

Kilduff, M., & Tsai, W. (2003). *Social Networks and Organizations*. London: SAGE.

Killworth, P., & Bernard, H. (1976). Informant Accuracy in Social Network Data. *Human Organization*, *35*(3), 269–286.

Klaster, E., Wilderom, C. P. M., & Muntslag, D. R. (2017). Balancing Relations and Results in Regional Networks of Public-Policy Implementation. *Journal of Public Administration Research and Theory*, *27*(4), 676–691. https://doi.org/10.1093/jopart/mux015

Klein, K. J., & Kozlowski, S. W. (2000). *Multilevel Theory, Research, and Methods in Organizations: Foundations, Extensions, and New Directions*. San Francisco: Jossey-Bass.

Koliba, C., Meek, J. W., & Zia, A. (2011). *Governance Networks in Public Administration and Public Policy*. Boca Raton: CRC Press.

Koliba, C., Wiltshire, S., Scheinert, S. et al. (2017). The Critical Role of Information Sharing to the Value Proposition of a Food Systems Network. *Public Management Review*, *19*(3), 284–304. https://doi.org/10.1080/14719037.2016.1209235

Koskinen, J., & Snijders, T. A. (2022). Multilevel Longitudinal Analysis of Social Networks. *arXiv preprint arXiv:2201.12713*.

Krackhardt, D. (1987). Cognitive Social Structures. *Social Networks*, *9*(2), 109–134.

Krackhardt, D. (1988). Predicting With Networks: Nonparametric Multiple Regression Analysis of Dyadic Data. *Social Networks*, *10*, 359–381.

Krackhardt, D. (1990). Assessing the Political Landscape: Structure, Cognition, and Power in Organizations. *Administrative Science Quarterly*, *35*(2), 342–369.

Krackhardt, D. (1994). Graph Theoretical Dimensions of Informal Organizations. In K. Carley & M. Prietula (Eds.), *Computational Organizational Theory* (pp. 89–111). Hillsdale, NJ: Lawrence Erlbaum Associates.

Krackhardt, D. (2003). Constraints on the Interactive Organization as an Ideal Type. In R. Cross, A. Parker, & L. Sasson (Eds.), *Networks in the Knowledge Economy. Oxford University Press, Oxford* (pp. 324–335). New York: Oxford University Press.

Krackhardt, D. (2010). Social Networks. In J. M. Levine & M. A. Hogg (Eds.), *Encyclopedia of Group Processes and Intergroup Relations* (pp. 817–821). Los Angeles, CA: SAGE.

Krackhardt, D., & Brass, D. J. (1994). Intraorganizational Networks: The Micro Side. In S. Wasserman & J. Galaskiewicz (Eds.), *Advances in Social Network Analysis: Research in the Social and Behavioral Sciences*. Thousand Oaks, CA: SAGE.

Krackhardt, D., & Kilduff, M. (1999). Whether Closer or Far: Social Distance Effects on Perceived Balance in Friendship Networks. *Journal of Personality and Social Psychology, 76*(5), 770–782.

Krackhardt, D., & Stern, R. N. (1988). Informal Networks and Organizational Crises: An Experimental Simulation. *Social Psychology Quarterly, 51*(2), 123–140. https://doi.org/10.2307/2786835

Lazega, E. (2001). *The Collegial Phenomenon: The Social Mechanisms of Cooperation Among Peers in a Corporate Law Partnership*. Oxford: Oxford University Press.

Lazega, E., & Krackhardt, D. (2000). Spreading and Shifting Costs of Lateral Control Among Peers: A Structural Analysis at the Individual Level. *Quality & Quantity, 34*, 153–175. https://doi.org/10.1023/A:1004759418226

Lazega, E., & Snijders, T. A. (2015). *Multilevel Network Analysis for the Social Sciences: Theory, Methods and Applications* (Vol. 12). New York: Springer.

Lee, J., Rethemeyer, R. K., & Park, H. H. (2018).How Does Policy Funding Context Matter to Networks? Resource Dependence, Advocacy Mobilization, and Network Structures. *Journal of Public Administration Research and Theory, 28*(3), 388–405. https://doi.org/10.1093/jopart/muy016

Lee, Y. (2011). Economic Development Networks Among Local Governments. *International Review of Public Administration, 16*(1), 113–134. https://doi.org/10.1080/12264431.2011.10805188

Lee, Jooho. (2013). Exploring the role of knowledge networks in perceived e-government: A comparative case study of two local governments in Korea. *The American Review of Public Administration, 43*(1), 89–108.

Leenders, R. T. A. J. (2002). Modeling Social Influence Through Network Autocorrelation: Constructing the Weight Matrix. *Social Networks*, *24*(1), 21–47.

LeRoux, K., & Carr, J. B. (2010). Prospects for Centralizing Services in an Urban County: Evidence from Eight Self-Organized Networks of Local Public Services. *Journal of Urban Affairs*, *32*(4), 449–470. https://doi.org/10.1111/j.1467-9906.2010.00512.x

Light, R., & Moody, J. (2020). Network Basics: Points, Lines, and Positions. In R. Light & J. Moody (Eds.), *The Oxford Handbook of Social Networks* (pp. 17–33). New York: Oxford University Press.

Lusher, D., Koskinen, J., & Robins, G. (2013). *Exponential Random Graph Models for Social Networks: Theory, Methods, and Applications*. New York: Cambridge University Press.

Marcum, C. S., Bevc, C. A., & Butts, C. T. (2012). Mechanisms of Control in Emergent Interorganizational Networks. *Policy Studies Journal*, *40*(3), 516–546. https://doi.org/10.1111/j.1541-0072.2012.00463.x

Markovic, J. (2017). Contingencies and Organizing Principles in Public Networks. *Public Management Review*, *19*(3), 361–380. https://doi.org/10.1080/14719037.2016.1209237

Maroulis, S. (2017). The Role of Social Network Structure in Street-Level Innovation. *The American Review of Public Administration*, *47*(4), 419–430. https://doi.org/10.1177/0275074015611745

Mayhew, B. H. (1980). Structuralism Versus Individualism: Part 1, Shadowboxing in the Dark*. *Social Forces*, *59*(2), 335–375. https://doi.org/10.1093/sf/59.2.335

McLean, P. (2017). *Culture in Networks*. Cambridge: Polity Press.

Medina, A., Siciliano, M. D., Hu, Q., & Wang, W. (2021). Network Effects Research: A Systematic Review of Theoretical Mechanisms and Measures. *(Working Paper)*.

Moher, D., Liberati, A., Tetzlaff, J., & Altman, D. G. (2009). Preferred Reporting Items for Systematic Reviews and Meta-Analyses: The PRISMA Statement. *Annals of Internal Medicine*, *151*(4), 264–269.

Monge, P. R., & Contractor, N. S. (2003). *Theories of Communication Networks*. New York: Oxford University Press.

Mosley, J. E., & Jarpe, M. (2019). How Structural Variations in Collaborative Governance Networks Influence Advocacy Involvement and Outcomes. *Public Administration Review*, *79*(5), 629–640. https://doi.org/10.1111/puar.13037

Nisar, M. A., & Maroulis, S. (2017). Foundations of Relating: Theory and Evidence on the Formation of Street-Level Bureaucrats' Workplace

Networks. *Public Administration Review, 77*(6), 829–839. https://doi.org/10.1111/puar.12719

North, D. C. (1991). Institutions. *Journal of Economic Perspectives, 5*(1), 97–112. https://doi.org/10.1257/jep.5.1.97

Nowell, B. (2009). Out of Sync and Unaware? Exploring the Effects of Problem Frame Alignment and Discordance in Community Collaboratives. *Journal of Public Administration Research and Theory, 20*(1), 91–116. https://doi.org/10.1093/jopart/mup006

Nowell, B., & Kenis, P. (2019). Purpose-Oriented Networks: The Architecture of Complexity. *Perspectives on Public Management and Governance, 2*(3), 169–173. https://doi.org/10.1093/ppmgov/gvz012

Nowell, B., & Milward, B. H. (2022). *Apples to Apples: A Taxonomy of Networks in Public Management and Policy.* Cambridge: Cambridge University Press. https://doi.org/10.1017/9781108987646

Nowell, B., Steelman, T., Velez, A.-L. K., & Yang, Z. (2018). The Structure of Effective Governance of Disaster Response Networks: Insights From the Field. *The American Review of Public Administration, 48*(7), 699–715. https://doi.org/10.1177/0275074017724225

Ofem, B., Arya, B., & Borgatti, S. P. (2018). The Drivers of Collaborative Success Between Rural Economic Development Organizations. *Nonprofit and Voluntary Sector Quarterly, 47*(6), 1113–1134. https://doi.org/10.1177/0899764018783084

Ostrom, E. (2009). A General Framework for Analyzing Sustainability of Social-Ecological Systems. *Science, 325*(5939), 419–422. https://doi.org/10.1126/science.1172133

Parsons, B. M. (2020). The Effects of Risk, Beliefs, and Trust in Education Policy Networks: The Case of Autism and Special Education. *Policy Studies Journal, 48*(1), 38–63. https://doi.org/10.1111/psj.12246

Payne, G. T., Moore, C. B., Griffis, S. E., & Autry, C. W. (2011). Multilevel Challenges and Opportunities in Social Capital Research. *Journal of Management, 37*(2), 491–520.

Perry, B. L., Pescosolido, B. A., & Borgatti, S. P. (2018). *Egocentric Network Analysis: Foundations, Methods, and Models.* Cambridge: Cambridge University Press.

Pfeffer, J., & Sutton, R. I. (2000). *The Knowing-Doing Gap: How Smart Companies Turn Knowledge Into Action.* Boston, MA: Harvard Business School Press.

Provan, K. G., & Milward, B. H. (1995). A Preliminary Theory of Interorganizational Network Effectiveness: A Comparative Study of Four

Community Mental Health Systems. *Administrative Science Quarterly, 40*(1), 1–33.

Provan, K. G., & Milward, H. B. (2001). Do Networks Really Work? A Framework for Evaluating Public-Sector Organizational Networks. *Public Administration Review, 61*(4), 414–423. https://doi.org/10.1111/0033-3352.00045

Provan, K. G., Huang, K., & Milward, B. H. (2009). The Evolution of Structural Embeddedness and Organizational Social Outcomes in a Centrally Governed Health and Human Services Network. *Journal of Public Administration Research and Theory, 19*(4), 873–893.

Provan, K. G., Beagles, J. E., Mercken, L., & Leischow, S. J. (2013). Awareness of Evidence-Based Practices by Organizations in a Publicly Funded Smoking Cessation Network. *Journal of Public Administration Research and Theory, 23*(1), 133–153. https://doi.org/10.1093/jopart/mus011

Putnam, R. D. (1995). Bowling Alone: America's Declining Social Capital. *Journal of Democracy, 6*(1), 65–78.

Raab, J., & Milward, H. B. (2003). Dark Networks as Problems. *J Public Adm Res Theory, 13*(4), 413–439. https://doi.org/10.1093/jopart/mug029

Raab, J., Mannak, R. S., & Cambré, B. (2015). Combining Structure, Governance, and Context: A Configurational Approach to Network Effectiveness. *Journal of Public Administration Research and Theory, 25*(2), 479–511. https://doi.org/10.1093/jopart/mut039

Ripley, R. M., Snijders, T. A. B., Boda, Z., Vörös, A., & Preciado, P. (2022). *Manual for* SIENA version 4.0 (version April 28, 2022). Oxford: University of Oxford.

Robins, G. (2015). *Doing Social Network Research: Network-Based Research Design for Social Scientists*. Thousand Oaks: SAGE.

Robins, G., Pattison, P., & Wasserman, S. (1999). Logit Models and Logistic Regressions for Social Networks: III. Valued Relations. *Psychometrika, 64*(3), 371–394.

Robins, G., Pattison, P., & Woolcock, J. (2005). Small and Other Worlds: Global Network Structures from Local Processes. *American Journal of Sociology, 110*(4), 894–936. https://doi.org/10.1086/427322

Sandström, A., & Carlsson, L. (2008). The Performance of Policy Networks: The Relation between Network Structure and Network Performance. *Policy Studies Journal, 36*(4), 497–524. https://doi.org/10.1111/j.1541-0072.2008.00281.x

Sarkar, A., Fienberg, S. E., & Krackhardt, D. (2010). Predicting Profitability Using Advice Branch Bank Networks. *Statistical Methodology, 7*, 429–444.

Schalk, J., Torenvlied, R., & Allen, J. (2009). Network Embeddedness and Public Agency Performance: The Strength of Strong Ties in Dutch Higher Education. *Journal of Public Administration Research and Theory, 20*(3), 629–653. https://doi.org/10.1093/jopart/mup018

Schelling, T. C. (1971). Dynamic Models of Segregation. *Journal of Mathematical Sociology, 1*(2), 143–186.

Scott, T. A., & Thomas, C. W. (2017). Winners and Losers in the Ecology of Games: Network Position, Connectivity, and the Benefits of Collaborative Governance Regimes. *Journal of Public Administration Research and Theory, 27*(4), 647–660.

Shrestha, M. K. (2013). Internal versus External Social Capital and the Success of Community Initiatives: A Case of Self-Organizing Collaborative Governance in Nepal. *Public Administration Review, 73*(1), 154–164. https://doi.org/10.1111/j.1540-6210.2012.02622.x

Shrestha, M. K. (2018). Network Structure, Strength of Relationships, and Communities' Success in Project Implementation. *Public Administration Review, 78*(2), 284–294. https://doi.org/10.1111/puar.12787

Siciliano, M. D. (2015a). Advice Networks in Public Organizations: The Role of Structure, Internal Competition, and Individual Attributes. *Public Administration Review, 75*(4), 548–559. https://doi.org/10.1111/puar.12362

Siciliano, M. D. (2015b). Professional Networks and Street-Level Performance: How Public School Teachers' Advice Networks Influence Student Performance. *The American Review of Public Administration, 47*(1), 79–101. https://doi.org/10.1177/0275074015577110

Siciliano, M. D. (2017). Ignoring the Experts: Networks and Organizational Learning in the Public Sector. *Journal of Public Administration Research and Theory, 27*(1), 104–119. https://doi.org/10.1093/jopart/muw052

Siciliano, M. D., & Thompson, J. R. (2015). If You Are Committed, Then so Am I: The Role of Social Networks and Social Influence on Organizational Commitment. *Administration & Society, 50*(7), 916–946. https://doi.org/10.1177/0095399715617987

Siciliano, M. D., & Whetsell, T. A. (2021). Strategies of Network Intervention: A Pragmatic Approach to Policy Implementation and Public Problem Resolution through Network Science. *arXiv preprint arXiv:2109.08197 [cs. SI]*. https://arxiv.org/abs/2109.08197

Siciliano, M. D., & Wukich, C. (2017). Network Formation During Disasters: Exploring Micro-Level Interorganizational Processes and the Role of National Capacity. *International Journal of Public Administration, 40*(6), 490–503. https://doi.org/10.1080/01900692.2016.1140200

Siciliano, M. D., Carr, J. B., & Hugg, V. G. (2021). Analyzing the Effectiveness of Networks for Addressing Public Problems: Evidence from a Longitudinal Study. *Public Administration Review, 81*(5), 895–910. https://doi.org/10.1111/puar.13336

Siciliano, M. D., Wang, W., & Medina, A. (2021). Mechanisms of Network Formation in the Public Sector: A Systematic Review of the Literature. *Perspectives on Public Management and Governance, 4*(1), 63–81. https://doi.org/10.1093/ppmgov/gvaa017

Siciliano, M. D., Yenigun, D., & Ertan, G. (2012). Estimating Network Structure Via Random Sampling: Cognitive Social Structures and the Adaptive Threshold Method. *Social Networks, 34*(4), 585–600. http://dx.doi.org/10.1016/j.socnet.2012.06.004

Snijders, T. A. B. (2017). Stochastic Actor-Oriented Models for Network Dynamics. *Annual Review of Statistics and Its Application, 4*(1), 343–363. https://doi.org/10.1146/annurev-statistics-060116-054035

Snijders, T. A. B., & Steglich, C. E. G. (2015). Representing Micro–Macro Linkages by Actor-based Dynamic Network Models. *Sociological Methods & Research, 44*(2), 222–271. https://doi.org/10.1177/0049124113494573

Tasselli, S., Kilduff, M., & Menges, J. I. (2015). The Microfoundations of Organizational Social Networks: A Review and an Agenda for Future Research. *Journal of Management, 41*(5), 1361–1387. https://doi.org/10.1177/0149206315573996

Thurmaier, K., & Wood, C. (2002). Interlocal Agreements as Overlapping Social Networks: Picket–Fence Regionalism in Metropolitan Kansas City. *Public Administration Review, 62*(5), 585–598. https://doi.org/10.1111/1540-6210.00239

Turrini, A., Cristofoli, D., Frosini, F., & Nasi, G. (2010). Networking Literature About Determinants of Network Effectiveness. *Public Administration, 88*(2), 528–550. https://doi.org/10.1111/j.1467-9299.2009.01791.x

Uzzi, B., & Spiro, J. (2005). Collaboration and Creativity: The Small World Problem. *American Journal of Sociology, 111*(2), 447–504.

Valente, T. W. (2012). Network Interventions. *Science, 337*(6090), 49–53. https://doi.org/10.1126/science.1217330

Varda, D. M. (2011). A Network Perspective on State-Society Synergy to Increase Community-Level Social Capital. *Nonprofit and Voluntary Sector Quarterly, 40*(5), 896–923. https://doi.org/10.1177/0899764010378171

Wang, C., Lizardo, O., & Hachen, D. S. (2021). Using Big Data to Examine the Effect of Urbanism on Social Networks. *Journal of Urban Affairs, 43*(1), 40–56. https://doi.org/10.1080/07352166.2018.1550350

Wang, P., Robins, G., Pattison, P., & Lazega, E. (2013). Exponential Random Graph Models for Multilevel Networks. *Social Networks*, *35*(1), 96–115. https://doi.org/10.1016/j.socnet.2013.01.004

Wang, P., Robins, G., Pattison, P., & Lazega, E. (2016). Social Selection Models for Multilevel Networks. *Social Networks*, *44*, 346–362. https://doi.org/10.1016/j.socnet.2014.12.003

Wang, W. (2016). Exploring the Determinants of Network Effectiveness: The Case of Neighborhood Governance Networks in Beijing. *Journal of Public Administration Research and Theory*, *26*(2), 375–388. https://doi.org/10.1093/jopart/muv017

Wasserman, S., & Pattison, P. (1996). Logit Models and Logistic Regressions for Social Networks: I. An Introduction to Markov Graphs and p*. *Psychometrika*, *61*(3), 401–425.

Wellman, B., & Berkowitz, S. D. (Eds.). (1988). *Social Structures: A Network Approach*. Cambridge: Cambridge University Press.

Whetsell, T. A., Siciliano, M. D., Witkowski, K. G. K., & Leiblein, M. J. (2020). Government as Network Catalyst: Accelerating Self-Organization in a Strategic Industry. *Journal of Public Administration Research and Theory*, *30*(3), 448–464. https://doi.org/10.1093/jopart/muaa002

Yi, H. (2018). Network Structure and Governance Performance: What Makes a Difference? *Public Administration Review*, *78*(2), 195–205. https://doi.org/10.1111/puar.12886

Yi, H., Berry, F. S., & Chen, W. (2018). Management Innovation and Policy Diffusion through Leadership Transfer Networks: An Agent Network Diffusion Model. *Journal of Public Administration Research and Theory*, *28*(4), 457–474. https://doi.org/10.1093/jopart/muy031

Ylikoski, P. (2016). *Thinking with the Coleman Boat*. The IAS Working Paper Series. Linkoping University

Zappa, P., & Lomi, A. (2015). The Analysis of Multilevel Networks in Organizations: Models and Empirical Tests. *Organizational Research Methods*, *18*(3), 542–569. https://doi.org/10.1177/1094428115579225

Cambridge Elements ≡

Public and Nonprofit Administration

Andrew Whitford

University of Georgia

Andrew Whitford is Alexander M. Crenshaw Professor of Public Policy in the School of Public and International Affairs at the University of Georgia. His research centers on strategy and innovation in public policy and organization studies.

Robert Christensen

Brigham Young University

Robert Christensen is professor and George Romney Research Fellow in the Marriott School at Brigham Young University. His research focuses on prosocial and antisocial behaviors and attitudes in public and nonprofit organizations.

About the Series

The foundation of this series are cutting-edge contributions on emerging topics and definitive reviews of keystone topics in public and nonprofit administration, especially those that lack longer treatment in textbook or other formats. Among keystone topics of interest for scholars and practitioners of public and nonprofit administration, it covers public management, public budgeting and finance, nonprofit studies, and the interstitial space between the public and nonprofit sectors, along with theoretical and methodological contributions, including quantitative, qualitative and mixed-methods pieces.

The Public Management Research Association

The Public Management Research Association improves public governance by advancing research on public organizations, strengthening links among interdisciplinary scholars, and furthering professional and academic opportunities in public management.

Cambridge Elements ≡

Public and Nonprofit Administration

Elements in the Series